/

Elias al-Musili

A Chaldean Priest's Journey to the New World in the 1600s

WEAM NAMOU

HERMiZ
PUBLiSHING

Copyright © 2024 by Weam Namou

All rights reserved. No part of this book may be reproduced or transmitted in any form or by any means, electronic or mechanical, including photocopying, recording or by any information storage and retrieval system, without permission from the author.

Library of Congress Cataloging-in-Publication Data
9781945371028

Namou, Weam

Elias al-Musili
A Chaldean Priest's Journey to the New World in the 1600s
(creative nonfiction)

ISBN (paperback)
ISBN 978-1-945371-02-8

ISBN (eBook)
978-1-945371-11-0

First Edition

Published in the United States of America by:
Hermiz Publishing, Inc.
Sterling Heights, MI

10 9 8 7 6 5 4 3 2 1

Books by Weam Namou

The Feminine Art

The Mismatched Braid

The Flavor of Cultures

I Am a Mute Iraqi with a Voice

The Great American Family
A Story of Political Disenchantment

Iraqi Americans: The War Generation

Iraqi Americans: Witnessing a Genocide

Iraqi Americans: The Lives of the Artists

Healing Wisdom for a Wounded World
My Life-Changing Journey Through a Shamanic School
(Book 1) (Book 2) (Book 3) (Book 4)

Mesopotamian Goddesses
Unveiling Your Feminine Power

Pomegranate

Little Baghdad
A Memoir about an Endangered People in an American City

The Onedia Man

Joseph Naayem
A Chaldean Priest's Story During the 1915 Genocide

Maria Theresa Asmar
A Chaldean Woman's Story During the 1800s

Contents

Books by Weam Namou iii
Author's Preface vii
Introduction xi
Historical Context xv
Chapter 1: The Start of the Journey 1
Chapter 2: Heading to France 6
Chapter 3: Traveling to Spain and Italy 10
Chapter 4: Journey to America 16
Chapter 5: The City of Cartagena 22
Chapter 6: Panama 25
Chapter 7: The Land of Peru 28
Chapter 8: From Guayaquil to Quito 32
Chapter 9: The Bullfight 42
Chapter 10: Mines of Gold 46
Chapter 11: Journeys and Dangers 48
Chapter 12: Elias' Journey from Piura to Trujillo 53
Chapter 13: Elias' Journey to Lima 57
Chapter 14: The Journey to Huancavelica 68
Chapter 15: The Town of Aguamanga 72
Chapter 16: Cuzco, Peru 75
Chapter 17: Coca 79
Chapter 18: Cruel Death of a Silver Miner 82
Chapter 19: Legend of King Inca 86
Chapter 20: Illegally Gathered Wealth 90
Chapter 21: Silver-Bearing Stones 93
Chapter 22: Tucuman and Buenos Aires 97
Chapter 23: The Deposed Viceroy 100
Chapter 24: Return to Panama 105
Chapter 25: Soloman's Island 107
Chapter 26: San Salvator, Guatemala 110
Chapter 27: Journey to Mexico 115
Chapter 28: Attack of the Pirates 120
Chapter 29: From Mexico to Baghdad via China 122
Chapter 30: Return to Europe 127
Chapter 31: Elias' Final Destination 131

Author's Preface

Elias Hanna al-Musili, a Chaldean priest from Mesopotamia (modern-day Iraq), is the first known Easterner to journey to America. He journaled his travels, which took place from 1668 to 1683. It is a treasure trove of wonder and discovery, but it is the lesser-known historical accounts and narratives beyond the standard European-centric explorations of the Americas.

Both the Spanish monarchy and notables of the court sanctioned his journey and made ready the provisions he needed. Pope Clement IX welcomed him warmly and granted him the authority to celebrate mass. He conducted the liturgy primarily following the Chaldean rite but would occasionally perform the mass according to the Latin rite as well.

Elias traveled with high-ranking ecclesiastical and government officials, which granted him status and access. He received excellent treatment, likely due to the possibility he could report on local authorities' performance. Elias seized the opportunity to fulfill his mission, probably hoping to spread Christianity to the New World and to return with silver and gifts to aid his home church in Baghdad. His religious affiliations, liturgical rites, and letters of recommendation from the Pope and Spanish Queen gained him privileged access throughout his journey. On the outward voyage, he was even assigned private quarters on the lead ship. These contacts, including inquisitors and governors, opened doors for him, even to Peru's restricted silver mines, which rewarded him handsomely.

On a guided tour in the Dominican Republic, I encountered a curious parallel when our tour guide introduced himself as "Obama" and referred to our group as the "Obama family." At first, when he said this in Spanish (he spoke seven languages), I assumed that the Obama family had visited this region at some point. Turns out he adopted the name "Obama" because people said he resembled the former U.S. president Barack Obama, even though he himself did not think Obama was particularly handsome. However, he used the "Obama" name and "Obama family" designation as a way to keep the tour group together and ensure no one got lost or separated. His real name was Victor, but he joked that his last name would be too difficult for us to remember. I can confirm this because I can't recall it myself!

"If you can't find me, just ask anyone on the street for Obama," he said. "Tell them you're with the Obama family and they'll know who you're talking about."

While the reasoning behind this was to keep the group together, it served as a reminder that the significance of names and identities can take on unexpected meanings in different cultural contexts—much like Elias' own Chaldean heritage played a pivotal role in shaping his extraordinary journey. Just as the tour guide's use of the "Obama" name took on unique meaning in the Dominican Republic context, Elias' Chaldean background was a key part of his experiences and how he was perceived during his travels.

Jesuit scholar Rev. Antoine Rabbat discovered the manuscript in 1905 in the library of the Syrian Catholic Church in Aleppo, Syria. That same year, he published it in *Al Mashriq* (The East), a monthly Arabic publication of the University of Saint Joseph of Beirut, under the title "The Journey of the

First Oriental to America." He omitted the seventeen chapters where Elias describes the history of America's discovery, its ancient rulers, and the conquest of Spain. Rabbat may have done so because the information was already known.

Over time, subtle distortions in newer publications emerged, diminishing the significance of Elias' Chaldean identity. With that, it's as if a part of his story has been lost. Elias' Chaldean heritage is an integral part of his journey, a thread woven into the very fabric of his experiences. To truly understand his story is to embrace the richness of his cultural roots.

Elias began writing an account of his travels to the New World while in Lima in 1680. However, the original handwritten manuscript of this travelogue has never been located. The British Library preserves the oldest manuscript, dated 1751, while the copy discovered by Antoun Rabbat in Aleppo is now held at the Vatican Library. Rabbat praised Elias' observations and experiences, claiming no other Eastern traveler's accounts had matched them.

Elias deliberately cultivated an exotic Eastern appearance as he traveled the world. Eyewitness accounts described him wearing a long black cassock and white priest's collar, likening him to a "Turk." Elias himself took pride in the magnificent beard he maintained throughout his extensive journeys. This striking visual persona left a lasting impression, with those who encountered Elias referring to him as a "priest from Babylon."

For almost 20 years, Elias lived a nomadic life, traveling between major cities in Europe and the Americas such as Rome, Naples, Paris, Lisbon, Madrid, Lima, and Mexico City. Eventually, he returned to Spain where he is believed to have spent his final years, although this is uncertain. In 1692, he prepared the prayer book of the Chaldean rite that was later published in Rome by the Propaganda Fide. It revealed his relation to the patriarch of the Chaldean church. His father was also a priest of the same rite.

Beyond reclaiming his true identity, I wanted to bring Elias' story to life for a new generation who embrace digital formats and audiobooks. This is more than just a retelling of Elias' travels. It's an invitation to step into his world, and to experience the wonders he encountered. Through a third-person creative narrative, we delve deeper into the societal, political, and religious landscapes that shaped his journey, allowing his story to resonate with a deeper meaning.

It's with a deep sense of love and respect for Elias al-Musili's legacy that I present this book.

Introduction

by Chaldean Scholar Rev. Gabriel Oussani

The following is a journal article published in the *Catholic Historical Review* in January 1918 by Chaldean scholar Rev. Gabriel Oussani who served at St. Joseph's Seminary in Dunwoodie, N.Y.

The Earliest Known Mesopotamian Traveler in America

An account of a journey into America, in the years 1668-1683, by the Rev. Elias Hanna, a Chaldean Catholic priest of the Diocese of Mosul, in Mesopotamia.

It was somewhat of a surprise to the writer a few years ago when he came across in the Arabic monthly, *Al-Mashriq* (The Orient), published by the Jesuit Fathers of the University of Beirut, Syria, a series of articles describing the journey of a Catholic Chaldean priest to America in the years 1668-1683. No one had ever suspected that a Catholic priest, hailing from the distant cities of Mosul and Baghdad, and as early as 1668, and with the explicit approbation of the Spanish government and the recommendation of the Holy See, should or could have undertaken such a long, arduous and perilous journey to the New World. It had long been the intention of the present writer to publish an English translation of this remarkable Arabic manuscript, but the difficulty of identifying the hundreds of Spanish and South American geographical and personal names, so carelessly transliterated and so badly disfigured in their Arabic form, deterred him from the undertaking. However, at the request of the Rev. Dr. Guilday, he submits here a brief sketch of the contents of the work in the hope that it may prove of interest to the readers of the *Catholic Historical Review*.

The manuscript in question was discovered in 1905, in the Episcopal library of the Syrian Catholic Church in Aleppo, Syria, by a Jesuit father, Antoun Rabbât, and published by him in the Mashriq. (Vol. VIII, pp. 821 ff., 875 ff., 931 ff., 974 ff., 1022 ff., 1080 ff. and 1118 ff.). It is about 8 by 6 inches in size, containing 269 pages, 21 lines to the page. The narrative of the journey proper occupies the first one hundred pages. From pp. 100-214 we have a short history, in 17 chapters of the discovery of America and a description of its inhabitants, customs, etc. The last part of the manuscript, viz., from pp. 214-269, contains the account of a journey to France undertaken in 1719, by a certain Said Basha, Turkish ambassador to that country. Our manuscript is not the original, but a fairly well-written copy made of the original by a certain Gabriel ibn Joseph Qurmuz, in the year 1819, and belongs to the Maronite Hanna ibn Diyab, of Aleppo.

The author of the journey was a Catholic priest of the Chaldean Church, of the diocese of Mosul in Mesopotamia. His full name (p. 447) appears as Father Elias, the son of Father Hanna, the Mausulite (i.e., from Mosul), and of the family of Beth-Ammûda.

Our traveler started his journey from Baghdad in 1668

with the avowed intention of visiting the Holy Land, and, after spending some time in the city of Aleppo, he sailed from Alexandretta to Italy. From there he journeyed to France, Spain, Portugal, Sicily, and again to Spain. Having obtained the proper credentials from the Holy See and from the Spanish government, he sailed from Cadiz to America and, after a voyage of fifty-five days, landed at Cartagena in South America. From there he traveled through Panama and almost the whole western coast, through Colombia, Peru, Bolivia, Argentina and Chile, whence he returned, in 1680, to Lima, in Peru. It was in this last city that our traveler composed the narrative of his journey, which forms the first part of the work. In 1680, he traveled through Mexico and Central America, where he spent a considerable time. In 1683, he started his journey back to Spain and Rome, where he was cordially received by Pope Innocent XI.

Of the author nothing else is known. The object of his journey, judging from the few vague allusions in his narrative, seems to have been that of collecting funds for the poor and needy churches and dioceses of his country.

Historical Context

Providing historical information about the development of Christianity in Mesopotamia is important for contextualizing Elias's journey as a Catholic Chaldean. The term "Catholic" began to spread to the Middle East, including Mesopotamia, as Christianity expanded in the early centuries. By the first century and second century AD, Christianity had established communities in the region, with missionaries and apostles, including Thomas the Apostle, playing key roles in this process. However, significant theological disputes arose in subsequent centuries that would shape the landscape of Christianity in the area.

One of the most notable figures in this context was Nestorius, the patriarch of Constantinople in the fifth century. Nestorius disagreed with established Church teachings regarding the nature of Christ and the role of Mary. The Catholic Church teaches that Christ embodies two natures: one divine and one human, affirming that He is both God and man. In contrast, Nestorius argued that Mary was not the Mother of God but merely the mother of Christ's human nature. This position directly contradicted the teaching of the Council of Ephesus in 431 AD, which asserted that Mary is indeed the Mother of God, encompassing both the divine and human natures of Christ. As a result of his views, Nestorius was excommunicated, leading to the emergence of the Church of the East, which included the Chaldeans, who separated from the Catholic Church.

In the sixteenth century, a significant turn of events occurred as Chaldean bishops, led by Mar Sulaka, sought reunification with Rome. At the time, Pope Julius III was the pontiff. Mar Sulaka opposed the hereditary patriarchal succession that had become commonplace in the Church of the East and advocated for a more unified leadership. In 1553, Pope Julius III ordained Mar Sulaka as patriarch, successfully reuniting the Chaldeans with the Catholic Church. Tragically, Mar Sulaka was later killed, but his martyrdom laid the foundation for the Chaldean Catholic Church of the East, symbolizing both the struggle and resilience of these communities in their quest for unity within the broader Christian faith.

The relationship between the Chaldean Catholic Church and the Roman Catholic Church was solidified in 1681, when the Chaldean bishops formally accepted the papal authority of Pope Innocent XI. This event marked a significant point in the integration of the Chaldean community within the wider Catholic Church, leading to official recognition and support from the Vatican.

Elias al-Musili
A Chaldean Priest's Journey to the New World
in the 1600s

Chapter 1

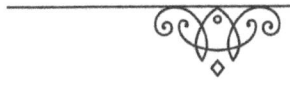

The Start of the Journey

Elias Hanna al-Musili was a humble Chaldean priest from northern Mesopotamia (modern-day Iraq). In 1668, he embarked on an extraordinary journey from Baghdad with Michael Condoleo, the head of the artillery department for Damascus, Aleppo, and Baghdad—regions under the Ottoman Empire. Born in Crete, Condoleo often traveled around the country to inspect the artillery depots, on orders from the Ottoman government. Missionaries described him as a devout Catholic who led a good Christian life. A wealthy and influential person, he was very helpful to the missionaries, both financially and culturally. The head of the Jesuit mission in 1646, Rev. John Amieu, praised him often in his letters. Condoleo had children whom he sent to be instructed by the Jesuit delegate to Damascus to receive a Christian education and learn Greek.

Together, Elias and Michael ventured forth on a less traveled road towards the holy city of Jerusalem. Midway through their expedition, on the day of the Resurrection feast, a group of nearly one hundred highwaymen ambushed Elias and his eleven companions. A fierce battle ensued, but the travelers, armed with their rifles, emerged victorious.

Continuing their journey, the two men reached Damascus, and then Elias pressed on to the Holy City of

Jerusalem. There, he felt honored to visit the sacred sites, and awed by their grandeur. From Jerusalem, he traveled to Aleppo and then to the seaport of Iskenderun, where he boarded an English ship bound for Europe.

During a stop in Cyprus, Elias made a pilgrimage to the tombs of St. Eliazar, his sister Miryam, and Martha. The French/Provençal version maintains that following Jesus' resurrection, these three figures took up residence in the suburbs of Marseille. They were later interred on a hill known as Sainte-Baume, which remains a popular pilgrimage destination for those seeking blessings. However, most modern historians dispute the truth of this claim.

The Greeks of Cyprus believe that the remains of Saint Eliazar are buried in their cathedral in Nicosia, not in Provence. Martha, sister of Lazarus and Mary Magdalene, is believed to have traveled to southern France after the crucifixion. She settled in Tarascon, where she died and was buried. Mary Magdalene is believed to have traveled to southern France after the crucifixion and lived her final years as a hermit in the Sainte-Baume Mountain region before dying and being buried there, in the Basilica of St. Maximin in Provence, France.

The journey then took Elias to the island of Crete, known as Quraytish, and onward to the Venetian-ruled isles of Zantiya, Corfu, and Cyphalonia. Elias and his party arrived in the renowned city of Venice after seventy days at sea. While the regular passage time was about thirty days, favorable wind conditions could reduce the journey to as little as fifteen to twenty days. But storms and required port stops meant the ships could sometimes take up to two months to complete the trip between Syria and Venice in the seventeenth century.

Just outside of Venice, the hospital called Ste Marie de

Nazaret held them in confinement, which was known as the "house of purification." In Christian cities during this period, there were customary quarantine procedures implemented out of fear of the plague. Travelers were required to undergo a forty-day quarantine period in a designated isolation facility before being permitted to enter the city.

People knew this quarantine facility as a "Lazaretto" in Italian and "Lazaret" in French. The name derives from the biblical figure of Eliazar (or Lazarus), who was associated with leprosy in medieval times. They used these quarantine sites as hospitals or confinement areas to isolate individuals with contagious diseases like leprosy.

The travelers completed the full forty-day quarantine period in this isolation facility. On the forty-first day, the head physician arrived to assess their health and look for any signs of illness. For those deemed healthy, he issued certificates allowing them to enter the city of Venice.

Elias spent the next twenty days exploring the wonders of Venice, especially the churches where he marveled at the magnificent St. Mark's Basilica, which was consecrated on October 8, 1094. Despite enduring significant challenges throughout history, including devastating fires in the eleventh and fifteenth centuries and Napoleon's suppression and looting of churches, Venice today boasts an impressive 139 church buildings within its compact six-square-kilometer area. Catholic churches make up ninety-six percent of the 139 churches in Venice, either currently or originally founded as such. Eighty-eight of these buildings remain operating churches that hold at least one weekly mass. The other fifty-one buildings have been converted into museums, schools, shops, or storage facilities.

After leaving Venice, Elias embarked on an odyssey that took him to Rome. There, he spent six months exploring the holy sites, with a special focus on St. Peter's Basilica. According to tradition, this basilica is believed to be the burial site of Saint Peter, the foremost apostle of Jesus and the first Bishop of Rome (Pope). This was the earliest organized Christian faith, from a historical and theological standpoint. St. Thomas spread a form of Christianity in Mesopotamia that resembled the early, decentralized version of the faith before the Catholic Church's institutional structure was established.

Elias' journey led him to the lands of Ferdinand II de' Medici, the Grand Duke of Tuscany. Ferdinand II reigned for almost fifty years, starting at the age of eleven after his father's death. People knew him for his interest in science, technology, and innovation. He helped Tuscany thrive during a turbulent period in European history.

From there, Elias traveled to the duchy's port of Livorno. The port had been developed into a major Mediterranean trading hub under the Medici Grand Dukes. Livorno had been transformed from a small fishing village into a cosmopolitan city with a bustling harbor, liberal policies that attracted merchants from across Europe, and an early model of religious tolerance that welcomed Jews, Greeks, and other minorities.

A few days later, Elias departed Livorno for the port city of Genoa, then ruled by an independent princely republic rather than a monarch. Genoa had a long and proud history as a maritime power, with its fleet of ships dominating trade across the Mediterranean for centuries. The city was renowned for its striking architecture, including the lavish palaces of the Genoese nobility that lined its winding streets. Its control of lucrative trade routes and operation of key banking and financial institutions that served much of Europe allowed Genoa to accumulate immense wealth, contributing to its reputation.

This independent princely republic, unlike other political structures in Italy, preserved its autonomy and prosperity despite attempts by Spain and France to gain control over the Italian states. Elias would have marveled at Genoa's striking skyline, its bustling harbor activities, and the financial prowess that had made it one of the richest cities in Europe.

Chapter 2

Heading to France

After disembarking at the bustling port of Marseille, Elias set out overland, making his way to the historic city of Avignon. Despite being in France, Avignon was under the Pope's administration. In 1348, Pope Clement VI from Anna, Queen of Sicily and Countess of Provence, officially purchased the city and its surrounding suburbs.

This purchase marked the beginning of Avignon's status as the papal seat, as the Roman popes would live in the city from 1309 onward, even before the official acquisition. For nearly five hundred years, Avignon remained under the direct rule of the papacy, with the city administered on the popes' behalf by an apostolic delegate. The era of Avignon as the "City of the Popes" ended in 1789. French revolutionaries took control of the city from the papacy during the events of the French Revolution.

Continuing his journey, Elias traveled upriver with his boat pulled by horses. Eventually, he arrived at Lyon, which is one of the most prominent cities in France, second only to Paris. During that time, Lyon experienced a period of immense prosperity and growth. What contributed to its greatness was the textile industry, bustling commerce, financial clout, architectural splendor, and intellectual dynamism. It maintained its status for centuries to come.

Elias met Francois Picquet, a pious figure who had served as a consul in Aleppo and was now a bishop in Lyon, at this location. During his time in Aleppo, Picquet was known for his piety, virtue, and tireless efforts to support Catholics and Christian missionaries in the region. Through his advocacy, he helped install Andreas as the Patriarch of the Syrian Catholics. His kindness and aid to those in need earned him widespread acclaim from both the clergy and common folk.

Upon returning to France in 1663, Picquet became the Bishop of Césarople and later Babylon. He also fulfilled the role of the Apostolic Delegate to Persia. King Louis XIV appointed Picquet as his ambassador to the court of the Shah. He spent the latter part of his life serving the Church and Christians in the East. He died in the Persian city of Hamadan in 1658.

With Picquet's warm hospitality and guidance, Elias pressed on, arriving at last in the magnificent city of Paris, the seat of the French King. Upon entering the city, he sought an audience with the victorious king and received a warm reception. He also visited the king's brother, the Duke of Orléans, offering him a sword as a gift and conducting mass for him in the church of his palace. Elias brought gifts that were fit for royalty, implying that the head of the Chaldean Church supported him in building connections with the Catholic establishment of Latin Europe.

All were exceedingly hospitable to Elias.

Elias' journey to Paris took place against the backdrop of ongoing tensions between the Ottoman Empire and Catholic Europe. The Ottoman ruler at the time was Sultan Muhammad IV, who reigned from 1648 to 1687. During Muhammad IV's turbulent rule, the Ottomans unsuccessfully besieged Vienna in 1683, a major turning point in the longstanding conflict between the Ottomans and the Hapsburg Holy Roman Empire.

Meanwhile, in France, King Louis XIV was on the throne,

ruling from 1643 to 1715. The French king had urged Sultan Muhammad IV to continue the war against the Hapsburgs, as Louis was himself engaged in his own struggles with the Hapsburg dynasty, although his mother was the Hapsburg princess Anne of Austria. This geopolitical context helps explain the warm reception Elias received from both the French king and the Duke of Orléans during his visit to Paris.

Then Elias delivered to prince St. Aignan a letter from his uncle, Padre John, the honorable Capuchin monk who headed the order in Aleppo. The prince received Elias with honor and generously because of his uncle, the padre. This Padre John was likely Rev. Jean-Baptiste de St. Aignan, a pious and virtuous Capuchin priest who served the church in Aleppo and Mosul for many years. It seems that he had close connections with the French government. His signature, along with other prominent clergy like Rev. Nicola Poirresson, was found on official dispatches to the Holy See and French cabinet.

Elias viewed the French court to be exceptionally welcoming, and during his stay in the capital, he witnessed an act of remarkable charity. A group of seventeen women, both virgins and widows, had renounced their worldly possessions, donating them to a renowned charitable organization known as the "Charité." These pious women, founded by Saint Vincent du Pau, had branches across the world and were celebrated for their virtuous acts and service to the poor.

Elias learned that the nuns carefully managed the endowments and donations left to their charitable society. Through wise investment, they earned a substantial two million units of currency, or twenty karras, in annual profit. They then distributed this money weekly to the poor, needy, churches, monasteries, the sick, and travelers, without regard for east or west. The nuns even used funds to help marry off the daughters of the destitute.

Witnessing the nuns' great works firsthand during his time in Paris, Elias was deeply impressed. While there, he also frequently visited an emissary, known as an Ilçi, whom Sultan Muhammad Khan had sent to meet with King Louis. Elias, knowing Turkish well, was able to converse extensively with the Ilçi, who urged him to remain in Paris rather than continue his journey. Elias ended up spending eight months in the French capital, learning and observing all that he could.

The piety and generosity of the Parisians left a strong impression on him. He continued his grand tour of France, excited to discover more of its splendor and delve into its rich religious heritage.

Chapter 3

Traveling to Spain and Italy

From Paris, Elias headed for Spain, following in the footsteps of countless travelers before him. He passed through the historic city of Orléans, a hub of French culture and learning, dating back to the Roman era. Then, Elias encountered a settlement he recorded as "Bonras"—a name that has puzzled scholars, as no such city seems to exist. Some suggest Elias may have mistakenly documented one of the three famous Loire River towns of Tours, Amboise, or Blois, all thriving centers along the crucial waterway.

Continuing on, Elias traversed the lush Poitou region, home to the mighty Dukes of Aquitaine, before reaching the bustling port of Bordeaux. There, he marveled at the grand projects undertaken by the "Sun King" Louis XIV, who had overseen the construction of a series of locks and canals connecting the Dordogne and Gironde rivers, unlocking this inland waterway to maritime trade.

Crossing into Spain, Elias encountered the fortified castle of St. Jean de Luz, a strategic French stronghold on the border. Passing over the river, he arrived at the imposing Spanish fortress of Fuenterabia, near the small town of Irun. From there, he journeyed to the thriving seaside port of San Sebastian, a gateway to the Iberian interior.

Along the way, Elias made pilgrimages to sites of great

spiritual significance. In Burgos, he visited an Augustinian monastery housing the revered "Cristo de Burgos"—a small cross said to possess miraculous powers. One of the most well-known tales dates back to the thirteenth century. It involves a group of thieves attacking a young pilgrim on his way to the shrine of Santiago de Compostela, leaving him to die. As he lay dying, he clasped the small crucifix and prayed fervently to Christ for mercy. The young man experienced a miraculous revival and could continue his journey, all thanks to the Cristo de Burgos cross that saved his life. Another legend tells of a group of Moorish soldiers who tried to steal the sacred relic from the Augustinian monastery. As they attempted to remove it, the Cristo de Burgos reportedly became incredibly heavy, resisting all their efforts. Terrified, the Moors fled, leaving the cross unharmed.

Elias also encountered a convent dedicated to Armenian nuns, and the tomb of a mysterious "King Ohanasi Taka," though records of such a figure remain elusive. Elias finally arrived in Madrid, the seat of Spanish power. He presented letters from Pope Clement IX to Queen Mary-Anne of Austria, the regent, who was the wife of the late King Phillip IV. King Phillip IV had passed away, leaving behind an infant son named Carlos II. The queen promptly issued him orders for a substantial sum of one thousand silver piasters. This amount was to be drawn from the colonial treasuries of Sicily and Naples, serving as a testament to the importance Elias' journey held for the Catholic world.

Leaving Madrid, Elias continued his Iberian odyssey, entering the rugged province of Aragon. As he journeyed northward, he arrived at the historic city of Zaragossa, a place of immense significance in Spanish royal history. Here, within the towering walls of the Aljafería Palace, the kings of Spain solidified their claim to the Aragonese crown by being crowned for centuries.

Elias sought an audience with one of the most intriguing figures in the Spanish court—Don Juan of Austria, the half-brother of the reigning monarch. Don Juan, a famous military commander and statesman, warmly received the traveling scholar. He was undoubtedly eager to hear tales of the scholar's lengthy route and the religious relics he had encountered.

Continuing towards the Catalan coast, Elias reached the thriving port city of Barcelona, a center of commerce and culture that had long been a rival to Madrid's power. Here, he boarded a stately vessel belonging to the King of Spain, ready to set sail across the waters of the Mediterranean. But after Elias' ship left the safety of Barcelona's harbor, fierce storms swept through the treacherous Gulf of Lyon, lashing the vessel with towering waves and howling winds. For twenty-five harrowing days, the ship took refuge in the small port of Cadaqués, its captain and crew powerless against the fury of the sea.

Once the weather improved, Elias and the ship's crew could finally depart on a Sunday, after holding mass. Following a full day and night at sea, they arrived at France's harbor in Toulon. From there, Elias traveled to Rome, where he visited his nephew, a deacon named Yunân, who had just completed his studies at the Propaganda Fide seminary and was preparing to return home.

Next, Elias went to Naples and presented the queen's order to her viceroy, who instructed him to travel to Sicily to collect the thousand piasters owed to him. Elias followed those orders. In Palermo, the queen's viceroy promised to reward him with a thousand piasters, but two months later, the viceroy informed him he could not fulfill his promise. Elias sent his nephew back to Aleppo, but he soon realized that he couldn't get the promised money from the hard-hearted viceroy, despite all he had endured to get to Palermo.

Resolute in his quest, Elias returned to Naples, hoping to collect the thousand piasters from the viceroy there. But once more, his efforts encountered disappointment. The viceroy dismissed Elias's claim, stating that since the governor of Sicily had not provided the funds, he too would not honor the original pledge. Dejected and penniless, Elias embarked on a journey back to Spain, traveling through Rome and the port of Livorno. He wanted to return to the queen her order. Upon reaching Zaragossa, Elias shared his harrowing tale with the brother of the king, who became moved by Elias's hardships and losses. These included four hundred piasters spent on his journey from Italy and back.

Joseph Fattal, a man from Aleppo who had made Rome his home, accompanied Elais back to Madrid to see the queen. When Elias presented his situation to the queen, she was deeply distressed by the rejection of her order. He returned her order and left for Portugal.

In Portugal, Elias encountered an intriguing figure—the imprisoned king of the Island of Terceira. This was Dom Afonso VI, known as "the Victorious," the second king of Portugal from the House of Braganza. Afonso VI had reigned for decades, although power struggles marked his early years on the throne. Initially, Afonso's mother, Luisa de Guzmán, acted as regent. However, Afonso later removed her from power in 1662 and placed her in a convent. He then took control with the assistance of his favorite, Luís de Vasconcelos e Sousa.

Afonso's reign saw the end of the Restoration War and Spain's recognition of Portugal's independence. He also negotiated a French alliance through his marriage. However, in 1668, Afonso's brother, Pedro II, conspired to have him declared unfit to rule and took de facto power as regent, although Afonso remained the nominal sovereign.

Afonso's wife, Queen Maria Francisca, later received an annulment and married Pedro. Though Pedro could not be officially crowned as king since his brother was still alive, he had a daughter with the Queen and wielded supreme authority. But they only allowed him the title of "prince."

Elias met with the prince and had a conversation with him. He spent seven months in Portugal and visited churches and monasteries. Among the inhabitants, he encountered fine and generous Catholics, as well as Christians of Jewish ancestry. He noticed this group didn't intermarry with old-Christians, and some denied Christianity. When the Inquisitions proved this denial, they condemned them to death by burning.

During the time, the Spanish and Portuguese Inquisition were active and targeted religious minorities, including Jewish converts to Christianity, known as "conversos" or "New Christians." They accused them of "judaizing"—maintaining Jewish beliefs and practices despite their conversion to Catholicism. The Inquisition was a judicial institution established by the Catholic Church to identify and punish heresy, especially among converted Jews and Muslims.

To understand the broader context, one needs to go back further in time. In 711 CE, Muslim armies from North Africa successfully conquered much of the Iberian Peninsula, leaving only pockets of resistance in the northern regions. For the next eight centuries, there was Islamic rule over at least part of Spain. The northern areas of Christian resistance were where the Reconquista originated. It was a long military campaign by Christian kingdoms in northern Iberia to reconquer the Iberian lands from Muslim rule. This process finally culminated in 1492, when the Catholic Monarchs Ferdinand and

Isabella conquered the last Muslim-ruled territory, the Emirate of Granada.

The Inquisition's zeal can be traced back to the historical context of the Reconquista. The experience of Islamic rule over the Iberian Peninsula likely influenced the Inquisition's ideology and approach. It led to suspicion of religious minorities and a desire for religious uniformity under Catholicism. The Inquisition also saw itself as defending Christendom against the perceived threat of the expanding Ottoman Empire, a major Muslim power.

The Inquisition officially ended in the nineteenth century, but its impact on religious persecution and discrimination against the descendants of Jewish and Moorish converts persisted for many more decades in Spain and Portugal. The relentless pursuit and executions of Jewish converts caused tremendous fear and suffering within the converso community. It was a dark chapter in the history of religious persecution in Spain and Portugal during this era.

Chapter 4

Journey to America

After spending seven months in Portugal, Elias returned to Madrid and took up residence at the estate of the Duke de Obro, who entertained him lavishly. One woman he met was the Marquesa de Losobles, who had played a role in the king's upbringing. She received Elias with great honor and requested that the king grant him permission to hold a mass for the royal family. A Roman deacon he had trained to assist him accompanied Elias. Entering the royal church, Elias conducted the mass for the king and his mother, the queen.

Afterward, the queen promised to grant any request and instructed Marquesa to ask Elias what he desired. Elias asked for time as he went to consult with his friends. They advised him to seek permission and a firm order allowing him to journey to the West Indies. The West Indies, at that time, denoted the Caribbean islands, which European powers such as Spain, England, France, and the Netherlands had colonized since the late fifteenth century. This region had become strategically and economically important to the colonial powers, serving as hubs for the lucrative Atlantic trade in goods like sugar, tobacco, and enslaved Africans.

This request surprised Elias, knowing that it was a challenging decision. It was difficult to get permission to travel to the West Indies as foreigners were usually not allowed without a direct order from the king. It was the papal nuncio in Madrid, Cardinal Mariscoti, who ultimately counseled Elias to make this request. Placing his trust in God, he made the request, and he received the necessary order through the queen, much to the delight of his friends.

The prince, in whose house Elias dwelt, made ready for him all that he needed for the journey and gave him letters of recommendation to some of his friends. The order of the queen carried recommendations to viceroys, bishops, priests, and all the governors of the "land of India" [Indies], urging them to lend Elias every support. Elias fortified himself in God and drew strength from His blessed mother, the Virgin Mary, and left Madrid for the old city of Cádiz, the port on the Atlantic Ocean. Elias reached it after a twelve-day journey by land and saw the ships to India all readied and prepared to sail. The bureau in charge of the realm's affairs was located in this port. Elias submitted to it the queen's order. They recorded it and issued him a secondary one to implement hers.

On February 12, 1675, Elias presented the order with the letters of recommendation to the "general of the galleons," Don Nicolao de Cordoba. He liked Elias and received him well and assigned him accommodation in his own ship. Elias placed his belongings in the cabin and closed the door. This galleon, a large multi-decked sailing ship developed in Spain and first used as an armed cargo carrier, was the lead ship of the fleet. Elias brought a deacon from Athens, as he couldn't find someone from his own people or religion in Cádiz.

Elias regretted deeply having sent his nephew Yunân to the lands of the East [homeland]. But regret at this juncture was to no avail. Some of Elias's companions warned that the Roman deacon would rebel against him and abandon him once they reached the "Indies.As anticipated, the deacon acted accordingly upon arrival. On February 12, they raised anchors and sails and set off. The galleons numbered sixteen. They departed to the sound of cannon fire and trumpets from the port, with flags fluttering and banners raised high.

Elias was among the travelers sailing away. Some were happy, others sad to leave their families behind. Such voyages to the Indies called Peru only happened every three years. The journey covered 1,500 farsakhs, each farsakhs equaling three miles, to the New World. The king's treasury was refilled there. Merchants loaded their galleons with goods to sell there. Only Spanish people were allowed to accompany them, by order of the king. These laws were in effect since Carlos V, the Spanish and Hungarian king who conquered the Indies. The galleons returned with great wealth—silver and gold worth twenty to twenty-five million, each piece valued at ten karats.

Three days out of Cádiz, a storm caused much disturbance for three hours. Among them was a nobleman, Don Nicolao Infante, the king's deputy, who died that night from intense fear. They tied a large jug to his feet and tossed him overboard so he would sink and be eaten by fish and not float again on the surface. They fired three cannon shots as he was tossed overboard because he had been appointed to head the government at Quito [Ecuador].

In another three days, they reached the island of Canaries, under Spanish rule. Sailing on, they encountered an English ship carrying about seven hundred black slaves, brought from Brazil to sell in the West Indies. Portugal had established permanent settlements in Brazil in the early 1500s and quickly began importing African slaves to work on sugar plantations. Over the next few centuries, Brazil became the largest importer of African slaves in the Americas, with most coming from West and Central Africa.

The Portuguese colony of Brazil relied heavily on this

forced labor to drive its agricultural economy, particularly the production of sugar, tobacco, and coffee. Brazil had the largest enslaved African population in the Western Hemisphere by the seventeenth century, reaching around one million by the end of the sixteenth century. Slavery in Brazil persisted until 1888, when it was finally abolished under Emperor Pedro II, making Brazil the last country in the West to end the institution of slavery. The reliance on slave labor was a key factor in slavery's longevity in Brazil.

As Elias and his crew neared the shore, the captain noticed a change in water color, indicating they had arrived at the Orinoco River flowing into the Caribbean Sea. Elias gazed out at the lush, unfamiliar landscape, taking in the sights and sounds of this New World they had finally reached.

Shortly after disembarking, the travelers were greeted by a local guide who introduced himself using his nickname "Obama" because, he said, his real name was too difficult to remember. He was a tall and thin black man with white hair. With a warm smile, Obama explained in English, with a Latin accent, that this region was part of the Spanish colony of Venezuela, known as the Captaincy General of Venezuela. "The Spanish have ruled these lands since the early 1500s, following the voyages of explorers like Columbus and Vespucci," Obama said, pointing towards Margarita Island. "This whole area has become an important hub of the colonial empire. You could say it's the jewel in the crown, if you'll pardon the pun."

Elias and his group liked this man. He was playful, witty, and very smart, but where was he from?

"Well, I'm a time traveler."

"What does that mean?"

"I come from Santa Domingo in the Dominic Republic.

I've travelled from a faraway land and also a different time, from the future to the past, so I can share with you important information."

Elias was still confused, and he observed the man. He had on a most casual and informal style of dress, a type of trousers made from a sturdy, woven fabric in a deep, indigo hue. This fabric was unlike any Elias had ever seen before. The trousers covered the legs fully, ending at the ankles, and were secured at the waist with small metal clasps. Elias, observing this curious attire, found the additional fastening mechanism—a strange contraption called a zipper—even more perplexing. To him, it seemed an odd way to secure one's garments. The man's white shirt was the most curious garment indeed. It was a short-sleeved upper body covering, flexible material akin to his own undergarments. Yet this was worn as the outermost layer, revealing the arms and a portion of the torso. The shape is simple, resembling the letter "T."

Elias thought, "What a most casual and informal style of dress, quite unlike the fine robes, cloaks and doublets we are accustomed to in our time. Yet I cannot deny a certain practical appeal to the simplicity and ease of movement afforded by these modern garments." The ingenuity of the people of the future amazed him.

"May I ask, Obama, what your family name is?" Elias inquired.

"Well, I'm not really Obama. That's just my nickname, inspired by a man who will be president of the United States in the future." He scratched his head. "So, Obama's full name is Barack Hussein Obama."

Elias raised an eyebrow. "Oh, so you are a Muslim man?"

"No, I'm Catholic. Obama identifies as Christian."

Elias frowned, clearly confused.

"You know what, Padre? Why don't you just call me by my real name: Victor."

Elias smiled, relieved to have clarity. He welcomed Victor to their group, and as they strolled along the coastline, Victor pointed out the shallow, warm waters renowned for their abundant pearl oyster beds.

"For over twenty years, the local divers have been retrieving large, high-quality pearls from these waters," he said. "There's even a legend that one day, the divers vowed to donate the first pear extracted that day to the church of the Virgin. But when they extracted a remarkably large and valuable pearl, they regretted their vow to the Virgin, wishing to keep the treasure for themselves. Determined to honor her, they decided to dive again the next day. To their astonishment, they recovered an even larger and more exquisite pearl. Driven by greed, they assured themselves they would fulfill their promise, but next time. So once again, on the fourth day, they dove as usual but surfaced empty-handed. From that day on, the ocean yielded no more pearls, leaving them to reflect on their choices."

Elias listened intently, fascinated by Victor's insights into the history and lore of this new land they had reached.

Chapter 5

The City of Cartagena

Elias and his group journeyed through uncharted lands for over a month and a half until they finally reached the bustling port city of Cartagena. As they approached the city, their guide Victor pointed out the strategic importance of Cartagena's location on the Caribbean coast. "This city serves as a key gateway for Spain's trade with its South American colonies," Victor explained. "The wealth that flows through here is truly staggering."

It was a Thursday during the holy week of Easter, and the group disembarked the next day, on Good Friday, eager to rest and recover from the arduous journey. Obama led them through the city, marveling at the towering cathedrals and monasteries. "Cartagena is a bastion of Spanish Catholicism in the New World," he said. "The presence of so many devout priests and faithful worshippers reflects the crown's mission to spread Christianity throughout these lands."

As they continued their tour, Victor's gaze suddenly brightened. "Ah, but you know, the most remarkable church in all the Spanish colonies can be found not here, but in Santo Domingo—the Cathedral of Santa María la Menor."

He went on, "This cathedral holds the distinction of being the oldest in the Americas, with construction beginning way back in 1504. Can you believe it? For over two centuries, the very bones of Christopher Columbus himself were interred within these hallowed walls." He chuckled, "I suppose you could say the good explorer never quite left the New World he discovered!"

Victor gestured animatedly as he described the cathedral's captivating architectural blend of Gothic, Renaissance, and Baroque styles. "Each detail, from the soaring spires to the elaborate rose window, was painstakingly crafted by master stonemasons," he marveled.

Falling silent for a moment, his expression turned wistful. "It's remarkable to think of all the histories these walls have witnessed—triumphs and tragedies, prayers and processions. This cathedral has borne silent witness to the unfolding of an entire era."

Turning to the group with a grin, Victor concluded, "So, my friends in the Obama family—sorry, I mean Victor family—if you're ever in Santo Domingo, come inside and let the ghosts of the past whisper their tales." You never know what secrets these ancient stones might reveal."

The governor, who had accompanied them, proved to be a gracious and hospitable host, welcoming the weary travelers with open arms. Elias and his group spent the next forty days immersing themselves in the vibrant culture and commerce of Cartagena. But their journey was far from over. Soon after, messages arrived from Lima, the capital of the Spanish viceroyalty in Peru. These messages summoned them to the bustling port of Portobelo, which served as a hub for trade between merchants returning from Peru.

"Portobelo has become the center of the trans-isthmian trade route," Victor informed the group as they made their way there. "Silver and gold extracted from the mines of Peru are shipped across the isthmus to this port, where they are loaded onto vessels bound for Spain."

The wait in Portobelo posed challenges for Elias and his companions. For two long months, they watched and waited as Peruvian merchants slowly brought in twenty-five lakhs of gold and silver.

Victor described the busy energy of the trade hub, with "Indians, Spaniards, and even bold French raiders all trying to get a share of the profitable trade." He laughed, "You'd think they would have learned by now that the real treasure is avoiding the dangers of this tropical place."

The group exchanged nervous glances at the mention of these "vampire-like creatures." Elias had heard tales of such beings back in the old country, creatures that could only be warded off by the power of garlic. He made a mental note to pack an absolutely massive supply of garlic before setting out.

Through forty arduous days of rain and sweltering heat, Elias and his companions endured. On their way to the port, they encountered a bustling marketplace filled with merchants selling various valuable goods like spices, silks, and precious stones from different regions. The air was filled with the cries of the vendors, each trying to entice passersby to purchase their merchandise. When the king's treasure finally reached the port, the general asked Elias to inspect the vast hoard of silver and gold. Its sheer magnitude left Elias awestruck.

Chapter 6

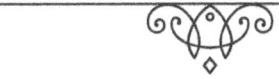

Panama

Elias' journey took him to the land of Santa Fe, where the precious emeralds were mined. However, the general in command of the fleet advised him against venturing inland, warning of the deadly poisonous snakes that claimed many lives, and the sheer distance of the journey. "I counsel you in the name of divine love," he said, "not to go, stray, and die in that country."

Victor nodded solemnly, adding: "The jungles of this region are treacherous, with untold perils lurking in the shadows. Many have perished attempting to reach the emerald mines, so it is wise to heed the general's warning."

Heeding the counsel, Elias refrained from the perilous trek and instead traveled with the galleons. Forty days later, Elias and his group departed Cartagena and headed for the port of San Filippe de Portobelo. They arrived at their destination after a twenty-day voyage and dropped anchor. Now, they were waiting for the ships from the land of Peru, which was also referred to as the Southern Sea or Mar del Sur.

Victor explained the strategic importance of Portobelo: "This bustling hub serves as the gateway for the transportation of the king's treasure and the merchants' goods between Panama and Cartagena. The wealth that passes through here is truly staggering." He described the town as delightful, situated about eighteen parsangs (an old Persian unit of measurement, three to four miles) from the port. The challenging terrain of mountains and forests straddled the two seas.

Elias marveled at the sheer magnitude of the king's treasury, which amounted to twenty-five million piasters, with each million equivalent to ten karats, and each karat worth 100,000 piasters. Victor noted, "Not all of this wealth returns to Spain—a significant portion is used to pay for soldiers, officials, and other expenses here in the colonies."

Portobelo, however, was infamous for its heat and disease. Elias also became sick but was cured by the Virgin Mary and the living Saint Elias, who shared his name. During this time, Victor, a faithful Catholic, gave him heart. He told him that he has found the light, Jesus. "Take solace in our Lord, my son," he said earnestly, "for it is through His divine grace that you shall be cured."

As Elias rested and recovered, he couldn't help but reflect on the duality of Victor's character. The man was playful and witty, occasionally using perverse jokes to lighten the mood. However, there was an undercurrent of unwavering faith that seemed to guide his every word and action. During discussions about religion and the divine, Victor's demeanor would change. He would furrow his brow with solemn concentration and speak with earnestness that bordered on reverence.

Elias could see that Victor's Catholicism was not just a superficial affiliation; it was a vital part of his identity, providing him with strength and comfort during difficult times. The man's ability to seamlessly transition between levity and gravity, humor and piety, never ceased to intrigue Elias. It was as if Victor possessed an uncanny ability to compartmentalize different aspects of his personality, switching between them with an ease that belied their apparent contradictions. Yet, Elias sensed that beneath this multifaceted facade lay a deeply principled individual, one whose faith was the steady foundation upon which all else was built.

Despite the challenges they faced, the merchants did not give up on their trade. The galleons were used to transport silver, gold, tiftik (a type of wool known as Vicuña), cacao, and other goods from Cartagena to the islands.

Elias made up his mind to join the merchants on their journey to Peru. However, the local governor advised him about a perilous grass that specifically endangered white European settlers, while the indigenous Indian populations remained unaffected. To demonstrate the peril, the governor sent an Indian servant to show the reverend firsthand. Elias claimed to have witnessed the grass suddenly spring up and move rapidly towards him, only to be halted by the Indian's shouts. Victor acknowledged the strangeness of this occurrence but cautioned that the governor may have had ulterior motives for discouraging Elias' travel.

Leaving Portobelo, Elias traveled for three hours along a small, rocky river before ascending a mountain to spend the night at a place called Burkarfon. The next day, he traveled to Chagres and then made his way to a town called New Panama. The original Panamanian capital had burned down the previous year in a devastating fire. Elias spent an extended period of time in the new town, where he noticed that the houses were primarily constructed from wood. During his stay, he formed a strong personal bond with the pious local bishop, Don Antonio de Leon, and the two even exchanged rings as a symbol of their friendship. The bishop even gifted the reverend the small cane he himself used.

Chapter 7

The Land of Peru

Elias then embarked on a ship sailing for the southern seas, known as the "Blue Sea" or Pacific Ocean, bound for the Spanish colony of Peru. The ship made a stop at Taboga, a small island near Panama. Elias met Captain Francisco, a man from Trujillo, who was the governor's brother-in-law.

Acting on the captain's suggestion, Elias and the rest of the group went ashore to stay overnight on the island. Yet, while being ferried on a small raft, it overturned in the dark waters. In the sea, Elias floated momentarily but clung to the raft using a cane gifted by a bishop. Miraculously, Elias and the others made it safely to the shore.

The journey continued along the coast after a three-day stay on the island for supply purposes. Elias found out about a dangerous whirlpool at sea called Gorgone, responsible for destroying numerous ships. Luckily, their vessel was able to navigate these treacherous waters without incident. Those who survived the perilous sea journey were seen as reborn.

Upon reaching the port of Santa Elena in modern-day Ecuador, Elias and his companions decided to continue their journey overland, rather than risk the perils of the sea. Elias listened to stories about the region's history from an elderly indigenous man in the port town. The elder shared stories of giant human remains in a nearby cave. Additionally, they discussed how the indigenous people were initially in awe and misunderstood the arrival of the first Spanish ships and horses in their land. The local people believed the large vessels were gigantic whales, and the tall masts were the creatures' wings. When they saw horses and their riders, they thought the two were a single, hybrid being—part animal, part human.

Intrigued, Elias took along twelve Indian companions who were well-armed, and they set out to the cave to verify the reports they had heard of giant bones being buried there. Inside, they found massive bones and skulls, with one tooth Elias extracted weighing nearly 100 measures. When they arrived, they lit the candles they had brought with them, fearful of getting lost inside the cavern. Elias led, sword in hand, with a man holding a light every ten paces to guide their return. As they proceeded deeper into the cave, they reached the spot where the giant bones were said to be buried. There they found the remains to be remarkably thick, and the skulls exceedingly large. Elias extracted a tooth from one of the skulls, which weighed nearly a hundred measures. He also examined one of the limb bones, finding it to be five hand-spans in length. An artist in a distant land later measured it and estimated the full height of the original body to have been twenty-five hand-spans.

Exiting the cave in wonder, Elias took the tooth as a remarkable memento of his journey through this little-known Spanish colony.

They went back to the port, hired mounts, and left with the Indians for Guayaquil. It's a seaport on the Blue Sea, four days away. The path led through dense forests and over small rivers.

In this region, Elias encountered a remarkable animal that resembled a dragon, known as the Caïman. He described it as a broad-bodied and measured five yards in length, with a mouth spanning about five fingers wide. Caimans are medium-sized crocodilians native to parts of Central and South America that are closely related to alligators. They have broad, flattened snouts and bony plates called scutes covering their backs.

There are several species of caiman, including the black caiman, spectacled caiman, and Yacare caiman, among others. They can grow up to five meters (sixteen feet) in length, though most are smaller. Caimans are apex predators in their habitats, which include rivers, lakes, marshes and wetlands. They prey on a variety of animals including fish, birds, mammals and other reptiles.

At certain times, they will emerge from the rivers and lie on the banks with their mouths open, presumably to get air. That's when small birds, according to Elias, entered the caimans' mouths. The birds pecked away at the dirt and debris embedded in the caimans' teeth, essentially cleaning them. Once the birds finished this "teeth cleaning" service, they flew away. Interestingly, the text mentions that the caimans appear to be pleased and welcoming of this behavior from the small birds. This intriguing example of interspecies cooperation in the wild, although likely exaggerated or fictional, is quite fascinating.

The Caïman emerges from the water and roams near the rivers. If it comes across a human or animal, it will lunge and swallow them whole, then rest on its hands. Its feet are like the paws of a lion. Elias witnessed the Caïman's predatory behavior towards horses and bulls at the river. The Caïman seizes them by the nose and drags them into the water, where other Caïmans assist in tearing the prey apart.

The local Indians devised clever hunting methods to deal with this formidable predator. They fashion a stick about half a yard long, sharpening both ends and hardening it in the fire until it is as sharp and hard as steel. One end is tied with a thin rope. When the Caïman approaches, an Indian will thrust this stick into its open mouth, embedding it firmly in the creature's flesh. The hunters then struggle to pull the Caïman from the water and flip it onto its back to immobilize it, before cutting it to pieces.

Another hunting tactic used by Indians involves a diver who enters the water with a rope. The diver loops the rope around the Caïman's middle and then swims to safety while his companions pull the trapped reptile from the river.

Many Amazonian tribes, such as the Waiwai, Zo'é, and Kayapó, continue to hunt caimans using harpoons, lances, and other handheld weapons. This requires great skill and bravery from the hunters. In some regions, hunters may use dogs to help locate and distract caimans, making them easier targets. The dogs do not directly engage the caimans.

Hunters also sometimes set traps near water sources frequented by caimans, using baited hooks or noose-like snares to capture them. However, commercial hunting and habitat loss have depleted caiman populations in many areas. As a result, some indigenous groups have shifted towards more sustainable practices, such as managing caiman populations on their lands.

In Brazil, laws now regulate caiman hunting and require permits. Commercial hunting is banned in many countries to protect vulnerable caiman species. Modern tools like firearms have also partially replaced traditional hunting methods in some communities, though the indigenous techniques still persist in more remote regions.

Tragically, Elias' party witnessed the Caïman's power firsthand when it swallowed a young attended to the local priest. He was so upset, he ordered the Indians to hunt the animal. They hunted two, cutting open the stomach of one and found the boy's body, to the great sorrow of the priest. They extracted the body and the priest had it buried.

Chapter 8

From Guayaquil to Quito

Elias and his companions reached the port city of Guayaquil four days after setting out. The town was inhabited by both Indigenous Indians and Spanish settlers. The locals, especially the Dominican monks, were exceedingly generous to Elias and his group.

After a ten-day stay, they left Guayaquil and traveled to the town of Baba, also home to a mix of Indians and Spaniards. Elias found the climate in Baba to be quite hot. There, he encountered trees resembling mulberry trees that bore a curious fruit—cacao, the key ingredient in chocolate. Elias observed the process of harvesting and preparing the cacao pods, which were then dried, roasted, and mixed with sugar, cinnamon, and ambergris to create chocolate patties. He noted that this chocolate was exported to "all Christian [European] countries" from Ecuador.

Victor, who was also in the region, provided some historical context on the cultivation of cacao: "The cacao plant is indigenous to parts of Central and South America and has been a crucial crop for centuries, sustaining indigenous communities." Long before the arrival of the Spanish, indigenous groups like the Mayans and Aztecs were harvesting and processing cacao beans to produce a rich, bitter drink that was highly revered. This rich, ceremonial drink was seen as a gift from the gods, a true source of spiritual nourishment. The Spanish conquistadors swiftly recognized the value of this crop upon their arrival, leading them to export cacao back to Europe. As a result, it became a delicacy favored by the upper classes. This kick-started the global chocolate industry as we know it today."

They journeyed from Quanalpo to Anbat. Elias was fascinated by the snow-capped mountains they came across. Among them was an active volcano that had recently erupted, resulting in ash, smoke, fire, and a plague that affected the local wildlife.

Victor noted the significance of the Andes mountains in the spiritual beliefs of indigenous groups: "These towering peaks have long held deep spiritual meaning for the Andean peoples. Many of the ancient civilizations, like the Incas, revered the mountains as sacred places, home to powerful deities and ancestral spirits. The dramatic landscapes and natural forces at work here have shaped not just the ecology, but the very cosmologies of the people who have called this region home for millennia."

Finally, they reached the town of Latacunga. It is home to a grand Carmelite convent that was built by the Bishop of Quito, Don Alonso de la Peña Monte Negro. The construction of the convent cost 250,000 piastres. Elias was greeted by four Dominican monks sent by their leader, who had heard of Elias's official orders from Rome.

Victor reflected on the clash between the Catholic Church and indigenous spiritual traditions. The arrival of the Spanish and the spread of Catholicism had an impact on the spiritual landscape of this region. However, it wasn't solely a story of suppression and destruction. The religious orders like the Dominicans and Carmelites saw it as their mission to incorporate elements of the indigenous belief systems into the new Christian framework. In many ways, they sought to find common ground and points of intersection between the old ways and the new faith.

He explained that certain sacred sites and rituals were repurposed or reinterpreted through a Catholic lens. And some indigenous practices, like the reverence for the Andean mountains, found parallels in Catholic veneration of saints and the divine creation.

"Of course, there were certainly instances of outright suppression and cultural erasure as well, but the story is more complex than a simple clash of civilizations," he said. "In the end, a fascinating synthesis emerged, where aspects of the ancestral spirituality continued to thrive, even as the dominant religion of the colonizers took hold. It was a dynamic process of adaptation and evolution, not just a one-sided imposition."

Elias listened intently, appreciating Victor's nuanced perspective on this delicate matter. It was clear the religious landscape of this region was a tapestry of ancient traditions and foreign influences, woven together over centuries of conquest and coexistence. But he believed, like many before him, that the Catholic Church was drawing in pagans lost in darkness, who worshipped idols, unto the path of salvation. And like others before him, he believed that St. Thomas the Apostle preached the holy gospels in South America and Christianized a number of its inhabitants. But times passed over what St. Thomas had taught about salvation, and it withered and faded away.

Elias' writings drew from a range of historical sources, including information on crosses, relics, and customs found in Central and South America. He also included reports of a great man who had visited indigenous groups in the past, taught them, and made predictions about their future.

Rabbat, the translator of Elias' work, claimed to have thoroughly examined travelogues, historical accounts, and mission correspondences. In his research, he discovered substantial evidence suggesting that Christianity had reached these lands and left enduring marks. However, the exact origins and dates could not be definitively confirmed. The customs and habits described, Rabbat argued, lent credence to the view that Christianity had become embedded within these regions over time.

Elias pointed out that Pizarro recounted an anecdote about his interaction with the indigenous people. The locals revealed that their forefathers had shared a remarkable account of two men who visited them—one tall with a light complexion, and the other short with dark hair. The Indians said the men's faces shone like the sun, and they preached with staffs in their hands.

The Indians showed Pizarro the location, indicating a spot fifteen parsangs from Lima, where they said the disciple had stood and preached. There, Pizarro found the prints of two feet on a rock. The Indians claimed they belonged to the disciple, though they could not read the faded letters etched into the stone. The Indians told him, "We do not know what has been written on this rock because we do not have an alphabet, nor do we read or write."

Elias reported that he had personally seen the drawings Pizarro had made of the mysterious footprints and inscriptions. The stories of St. Thomas' preaching in the Americas had persisted through the generations. They were passed down among the indigenous peoples even as the Catholic faith took hold in the region. Elias was familiar with the writings of Gregorious Garcia, a teaching monk. In Garcia's work, he recounted the story of the Indians of this land who shared with him about a cross brought by Thomas the Apostle. According to them, Thomas was able to walk on water as if it were land. Some claim he held mass, then left afterward heading east and did not return. This and many accounts by other eyewitnesses are included in Elias' writings.

Just two hours into his stay at the Monastery of the Dominicans, the city's governor heard of Elias' arrival and promptly visited him. The governor was angry and rebuked Elias for staying at the monastery. Elias calmly explained, "You know, my dear, that the monks had gone out to meet me, some two stages away, and escorted me to their monastery. You should speak first with the head of the monastery, and then take me to your palace."

The monastery head opposed Elias leaving, but they negotiated and agreed. Elias would spend the day with the governor, dine with him, then return to the monastery for the evening and stay in his cell with his attendant. The governor was Elias' old friend, having traveled from Spain on the same ship. Whenever Elias was offered delectable food on the ship, he would share it with the governor, and the two had become close companions.

The city where the bishop resided was rich in possessions, adorned with churches and monasteries. However, the bishop himself was known to be rather miserly and lacking in generosity. Poor water quality in this town caused goiters to develop in both Indians and Spaniards.

Victor and Elias talked about the intricate connection between the Catholic Church and colonial authorities in South America. They explored how religious orders like the Dominicans and Carmelites set up missions, convents, and churches during the Spanish colonization of the region. However, this relationship was often fraught, as the Church leadership and colonial administrators frequently clashed over power, resources, and the treatment of indigenous peoples. Navigating these tensions was a constant challenge for both the clergy and civil authorities."

During his two-month stay in the city, Elias had an interesting encounter regarding a molar tooth he had extracted from the bones of giants in the cave of Santa Elena. One of Elias' friends had a daughter in a convent, and he begged Elias to let him show the tooth to her. Elias obliged, but as the tooth was passed from one nun's hand to another, it mysteriously disappeared, and Elias was unable to recover it. The bishop imposed a sanction, demanding the tooth's production, but without success.

There was a nun in this convent who had bleeding for eight years. When the bishop hosted Elias, he asked about the benefits of the water extracted from a certain type of cane. Elias mentioned that he had learned from books about the potential benefits of this cane's juice for bleeding patients. The bishop asked Elias to provide some to the afflicted nun, and after drinking it for seven days, she was cured of her ailment.

Elias also learned about the textile manufacturing in this town, which produced woolen cloth like the renowned "Londra cloth" from England and southern France. He was also told of a nearby mountain that had been emitting fire and thunder-like explosions for years, violently expelling burning stones over forty parsangs. It was likely Mount Pichincha, a volcano near Quito, Ecuador. In 1660, it experienced a highly explosive eruption that sent plumes of ash and debris raining down on the surrounding area. This violent volcanic event caused significant damage, burning and destroying everything in the immediate vicinity of the mountain.

Victor brought up the Andes' long history of volcanic activity, emphasizing that it is one of the most geologically active mountain ranges worldwide. Throughout history, the region has witnessed multiple violent volcanic eruptions. These eruptions have had profound impacts on the indigenous communities living in the shadow of these mountains, destroying crops, homes, and infrastructure. At the same time, the rich volcanic soils have also supported thriving agricultural societies for centuries. Managing the risks and benefits of living alongside these dynamic geological forces has been a constant challenge for the people of the Andes."

Elias discovered an intriguing story about a buried icon of the Virgin Mary. The farmer, an Indian, took it to his home and hid it in a chest, but it reappeared back in the field. He repeatedly tried to keep the icon in his home, but it would miraculously reappear back in the field. The bishop was informed and received the icon with great reverence, building an honorable church to house it, known as the Church of the Virgin Mary of Jacicua. Visitors flocked to see the icon, and during plague outbreaks, it was paraded to Quito for nine days, curing the town. Then, she would be brought back to the church.

Elias was told of a river located twenty-four parsangs from the town, which when overflowing, would cast out sand mixed with gold from the heart of the mountain. Although he wanted to, Elias did not personally venture to witness this, as he was advised the road was too difficult. But he did manage to acquire some of the gold in the city of Quito.

After his two-month stay in Quito, Elias set out for the town of Otavalo, where a line referred to in astronomy as Linea (equator) passes through it. He observed the inhabitants lacked color and had swollen bellies. In this area, he was told that dead birds would fall from the sky on certain days. The trees were the only source of shade, as the sun never set.

Elias heard tales of non-Christian Indians living twenty-five parsangs from Quito. Priests who had come out from Spain sought to convert the local populations to Catholicism. During their travels, they encountered cinnamon, a highly valuable spice that was indigenous to parts of India and Sri Lanka. Recognizing its worth, the priests brought back cinnamon tree cuttings or seeds with them, likely hoping to cultivate the spice in the new colonies. However, the local Indian populations were protective of this economically important resource and did not want the Spaniards to discover the true origins of the cinnamon tree.

The cinnamon buds and shoots the Spaniards introduced were foreign to the indigenous peoples of the Americas, who were unfamiliar with how to properly grow and harvest the spice. This sparked tensions, as the colonizers sought to exploit the cinnamon trade while the native populations resisted these efforts to control their local resources. Additionally, Elias discovered that the local Indian populations in certain parts of Asia collected nutmeg. They would then send it to Caracas to sell to the English and Dutch, rather than the Spaniards.

Victor concluded, "The story of cacao, cinnamon, and other valuable crops in this region underscores the complex web of cultural, economic, and ecological exchanges that characterized the colonial era. Indigenous communities fought to maintain control over their traditional resources and knowledge, even as the Spanish sought to exploit them for profit and convert the locals to Christianity. Unraveling this history is crucial to understanding the lasting impact of colonialism in South America."

Then he cleared his throat and shared in a livelier tone the story of Fray Antonio de Montesinos, a Spanish Dominican friar who lived in the early sixteenth century. Montesinos is known for his impassioned sermon defending the rights of the indigenous peoples of the Americas. In 1511, Montesinos was stationed in the Spanish colony of Hispaniola, which is modern-day Dominican Republic and Haiti. At the time, the Spanish colonists were heavily exploiting and mistreating the native Taíno people, forcing them into slavery and subjecting them to horrific conditions.

On the fourth Sunday of Advent in 1511, Montesinos boldly condemned the abuses of the colonial governor and Spanish settlers in a fiery sermon. He emphasized that the Taíno people are human beings, not beasts or straw figures. This sermon caused an uproar among the colonists, who were unused to being challenged on their treatment of the indigenous population. But Montesinos refused to back down, continuing to speak out against the oppression and injustice he witnessed.

Montesinos' courageous stand is considered one of the earliest examples of the defense of human rights in the Americas. His sermon paved the way for the development of the "Valladolid debate" in Spain, where the rights of indigenous peoples were hotly debated. Though he faced backlash and even threats, Montesinos remained committed to his principles until the end of his life. He's remembered today as a pioneering advocate for human rights and a champion of the oppressed.

As a Chaldean priest, Elias must have had a deep respect and reverence for Fray Antonio de Montesinos' courage in defending the indigenous people in the Spanish colonies. Being a member of the Christian community in Mesopotamia, he would have firsthand knowledge of the struggles faced by minority religious and ethnic groups under foreign powers. The parallels between the Taíno people's plight and the challenges faced by Chaldeans and other minorities in the Middle East would not have been lost on him.

Moreover, Elias would have admired Montesinos' unwavering moral courage in speaking truth to power, even at great personal risk. A priest himself, he would have recognized the importance of using one's position and platform to advocate for the most vulnerable and marginalized members of society.

He may have experienced a sense of kinship with the Spanish colonists. This could be attributed to their shared Christian faith and the complex dynamics of colonial expansion and power struggles between the colonizer and the colonized. He may have empathized with their perspective, even as he condemned their unjust actions.

Chapter 9

The Bullfight

As Elias made his way from Quito to Riobamba, he was welcomed warmly by the Dominican monks. Holding mass at their monastery, he paid attention to the similarities between their rituals and his own Chaldean traditions, much to the delight of the brothers.

During his eight-day stay, he was visited by Victor, who wanted to continue being his tour guide. He was, after all, an indigenous man with deep knowledge of the region. "Welcome to Riobamba, my friends!" he said. "This city has a rich and fascinating history that I'm excited to share with you today."

Riobamba is located in what is now Ecuador, but in the seventeenth century, it was a settlement within the Audiencia of Quito, under the jurisdiction of the Viceroyalty of Peru controlled by the Spanish crown. Before the Spanish arrived, the Quechua or Inca cultural traditions occupied the area with belief systems for natural elements, ancestor worship, and rituals tied to agricultural cycles.

"Now, I know you might be wondering—where does the name 'Riobamba' come from? Well, let me tell you. It's a combination of the Spanish word 'rio' meaning river, and the Quechua word 'rispampa' which means 'plain.' So Riobamba literally translates to 'river plain.' Pretty fitting for this beautiful valley setting, don't you think?"

Before the Spanish arrived, this region was home to the indigenous Puruhá people. They put up quite a fierce resistance when the mighty Inca Empire tried to expand northward into their territory in the late 1400s. In fact, the Inca ruler Huayna Capac had to make an alliance with another local group, the Schyris or Caran-Quitu, in order to pacify the Puruhá and their leader, Condorazo.

"Can you imagine the power struggles and political maneuverings that must have been happening back then?" Victor asked. "It's a complex history, my friends, but an important part of Riobamba's story."

After the Spanish conquest, Riobamba was officially founded in 1534 by the conquistador Diego de Almagro. It became part of the newly established Royal Audience of Quito, under Spain's colonial rule. The city faced its fair share of challenges over the centuries—an earthquake in 1797 destroyed the original settlement, forcing the city to be rebuilt a few pasangs away.

"But through it all, Riobamba persevered," Victor told Elias. "In the 1600s, the people of Riobamba were a wealthy and noble lot. Just wait until you see the beautiful Spanish colonial architecture, the interesting buildings and graceful churches that gives the city its unique character."

Continuing south towards Cuenca, Elias and Victor encountered a curious scene in the Paramo mountains. "Look there," Victor said, pointing to the indigenous people paddling small boats down the rushing rivers.

Suddenly, a commotion erupted from nearby. A group of armed indigenous men emerged, shouting in a strange, rough language. They rushed toward a caravan of Spanish traders. The traders had a variety of goods including fine clothes, wine barrels, and crates of exotic spices. The Spanish traders scattered in a panic, some abandoning their precious cargo in their haste to flee, afraid of being killed.

The natives swarmed the abandoned wares, rifling through the crates and bundles. They selected the items they desired—lengths of vibrant fabric, earthenware jars, bundles of fragrant herbs. To the Spaniards' surprise, the Indians left behind small piles of glittering gold nuggets and coins as payment for the goods they took. As quickly as they had appeared, the raiders disappeared back into the dense forest, leaving the disheveled and shaken traders to collect what remained of their merchandise.

"When Spanish traders pass by, the natives will sometimes take what they need, leaving gold as payment," said Victor. "They know these lands better than any outsider."

The trek to Cuenca was no easy one, with the biting cold cutting to the bone. But Victor assured Elias, "Our people are resilient. We've lived in these mountains for generations." Upon reaching the town, Elias fell ill and was cared for by the local doctors.

"It was the Virgin Mary who restored my health," Elias told Victor.

The Cuenca governor, a friend of Elias, then arranged a "Fiesta de los Toros"—a grand bullfighting spectacle—to lift the traveler's spirits.

"Ah yes, the bullfights," Victor mused. "A celebrated tradition throughout Spain during the season. Though I must say, the tables are sometimes turned, and the bull's strength proves too much for horse and rider."

Elias listened intently, grateful for Victor's insights into the customs and rituals of this new land. "There is much to be learned here," he thought, his appreciation for the indigenous people growing with each passing day.

Bullfighting is still allowed in parts of Ecuador, but it

is a controversial issue there. The tradition has its roots in Ecuador's Spanish colonial past, but bullfighting events are now mainly held in the coastal and central highland regions of the country. However, the government of the capital region, Pichincha, banned bullfighting events within its borders in 2012. This was in response to growing public opposition to the practice, which many see as cruel to the animals.

Some other towns and cities in Ecuador have also held votes on whether to restrict or completely ban bullfighting. The results of these votes have been mixed—some places have prohibited it, while others continue to host the events.

Animal rights activists have pushed for a nationwide ban on bullfighting in Ecuador. While this has not happened yet at the federal level, the cultural importance of bullfighting seems to be declining, especially among younger Ecuadorians.

This shifting legal and social landscape around bullfighting has had economic impacts as well. The events and the tourism they attract have become less reliable sources of revenue for some communities. The future of this traditional practice in Ecuador is uncertain as the debate persists. If Elias were alive, he might view the bans on bullfighting as a positive step, reflecting increasing societal awareness and concern for animal welfare. As a man of faith, he may believe that traditions involving cruelty to animals are not aligned with principles of compassion and respect for life.

Chapter 10

Mines of Gold

After departing from his previous destination, Elias set out towards the town of Loja. The journey proved to be a challenging one, as he and his caravan encountered relentless rain for three days straight. Upon reaching Loja, Elias and his companions spent a day and night there, taking shelter from the intense cold and heavy downpours.

The following day, Victor came to meet them. He said, "Padre, the road to Loja can be real tough with all this rain we've been having. But the folks in Loja, they're used to dealing with the weather. You must be extremely interested in this land to take this trip. If you were another person, with a wife and all, well… I'd have to wish you lots of luck."

The following day, Elias continued his trek, heading towards the village of Zaruma and the nearby mountains where a gold mine was located. The path through the mountains was arduous, but after three days of travel, they finally reached the remote, mountain-top settlement of Zaruma.

Once there, Elias closely examined the intricate processes involved in extracting gold from the rocks. First, the ore-rich stones were brought up from the mine and meticulously ground into a fine powder using a water-powered mill. The pulverized material was then washed and sifted, with the precious gold flakes carefully separated from the dirt and debris. Finally, the gleaming metal was smelted and cast into ingots.

"Impressive, isn't it?" Victor said, joining Elias as he observed the sophisticated gold-mining techniques. "Our people have truly mastered the art." Impressed by what he had seen, Elias purchased a substantial quantity of the locally produced precious metal.

As he prepared to return home, a local priest advised an alternative route, one that was better but passed through a desolate, uninhabited region without any villages. Take with you provisions to last five days."

Elias consulted with his group, then decided to take the priest's advice. He assembled a small caravan, including an Indigenous guide and a mestizo muleteer. With the new guide, they no longer needed Victor so they said their goodbyes. Victor's brow furrowed with concern. "Five days in the wilderness, Padre? That's no small feat." He placed a hand on Elias' shoulder. "But I know you're up for it. Just be sure to pack well and watch out for any mischievous spirits that might try to lead you astray."

Elias did not display much emotion in return. This was his demeaner during most of his travels, his reserved nature a reflection of common cultural norms for Middle Eastern travelers of that era.

The group set out to brave the unknown.

Chapter II

Journeys and Dangers

Elias embarked on a challenging journey, traveling for a full day and night along a treacherous mountain road. The devil tempted the muleteer, and he plotted to take Elias's life. However, Elias's servant uncovered the muleteer's wicked intentions, and Elias promptly disarmed him, remaining vigilant for his own safety.

They reached a cluster of three villages—Basilica, Junjunama, and Vacanama—where the largely indigenous inhabitants were perplexed by Elias's appearance. The local bishops were also indigenous, like the people themselves. Notably, the Indians of the region lacked beards, save for a few sparse hairs on their jaws, so Elias's full beard was a source of great wonder and admiration. They thought he was either a prophet or a saint and told him he was very brave to have journeyed to this country.

The next day, they continued their journey towards the village of Amotapé. One night, as Elias slept in the tent, Elias's two companions conspired to kill him. Fortunately, a young Spanish-speaking Indian lad overheard their plot and, trembling, rushed to Elias' tent, woke him up, and alerted him of their plot.

That same night, one of the mules broke loose and headed toward the mountains. The mestizo went after him and didn't return until morning. During that time, Elias disarmed his would-be assailants of all their weapons. He took one of their swords in hand and called over the mestizo. "Get down on your knees and tell me how the devil tempted you with such a thought," he told him. "Confess the whole truth."

The mestizo confessed, pleading that Elias would absolve and forgive him.

Five days later, they reached another village, where the two treacherous companions fled in fear before they could enter. They left their mules behind. The local priest, who had lost his own brother along that perilous road, welcomed Elias with great respect and gratitude for his safe passage. "God delivered you from their evil," he said.

Crossing the nearby Rio Colan, which was teeming with large fish reminiscent of the Tigris River, Elias arrived in the town of Colan and stayed with the priest. The night before the Feast of St. Jacob, the priest asked Elias to lead the mass the next day. In return, the priest offered Elias all the donations made during the service.

Elias conducted the mass, which was attended by a congregation of four thousand indigenous people. After mass, he blessed the bread, then sat and greeted the parishioners. Elias was astonished to collect approximately 250 pesos as people came forward for the blessed bread and made their offerings.

Continuing his journey, Elias al-Musili soon found himself in the town of Piura, located along the banks of a river. Elias, aware of the difficulties of horseback travel in the hot and sandy terrain, wisely asked the governor of Piura for a tahtiravan—a hand-carried litter or palanquin—for himself and his companions. The governor readily obliged, ensuring the travelers' comfort.

Upon arriving in Piura, Elias was warmly received by the governor and alighted at his residence. He soon heard from the people a captivating local legend, one that spoke to the allure and peril of uncovering buried treasure. Fifteen years prior, the tale went, there lived a wealthy indigenous noble, known as a Kasiki, who had a single daughter as his heir. One day, while the Kasiki was away, his daughter encountered a man dressed in humble, paltry attire. Intrigued by his poverty, the young woman proposed a deal. If he kept her secret, she would show him her father's hidden gold in a remote cave outside the town.

True to her word, the daughter blindfolded the man and guided him to the cave's entrance. There, she loaded him with as many gold nuggets as he could carry, before returning him to the outskirts of Piura and releasing him from the blindfold. However, upon the Kasiki's return, he went to the cave and saw her footprints at the entrance of the cave. Realizing his daughter's actions, he poisoned her. The Kasiki himself soon after died as well, and to this day, the fabled cave of gold remains undiscovered.

The town, Elias observed while having tea at a café, was inhabited by both Spaniards and prosperous indigenous people, and boasted both ornate and more modest churches. He was there that Victor reappeared. He wanted to show Elias the Cathedral of Piura. "It's truly a sight," he said. "Come on, let me show you!"

Elias finished drinking his tea and followed Victor.

"Built in 1588, this cathedral has witnessed many important events in Piura's history. It was here that notable figures such as Miguel Grau, Ignacio Merino, and Carlos Augusto Salaverry were baptized. The cathedral houses numerous works of artistic and historical value, making it a true cultural treasure."

Elias appreciated Victor taking him this cathedral, but before he could ask some questions, Victor cleared his throat and put on a charming smile. "But the most historical church of all is the Cathedral of Santa Maria la Menor. It's in Santa Domingo which is..." He squinted and pointed north. "By land or sea, approximately 3,500 miles through Central America and crossing the Caribbean Sea."

Victor explained that Santa Maria la Menor was built in the early 1500s. It was the headquarters of the Catholic Church in the Americas and had a special connection to Christopher Columbus, one of the most famous names in history. His own son, Diego, was the one who laid the first stone to get this place started. "Talk about keeping it in the family, am I right?" Victor winked, playfully. "Now, you might be thinking, 'Victor, aka Obama, what do you know about churches? Aren't you supposed to be, I don't know, running a country or something?' Well, let me tell you, I'm a man of many talents and I'm a devout Catholic. In my country, the Dominic Republic, you have people of all backgrounds and skin color—blacks, whites, browns. But the one thing that unites them is the Christian faith."

Elias nodded, intrigued. He then sadly reflected that his own birthland, Mesopotamia, was once like that. Mesopotamia gradually transitioned from a Christian region to a Muslim one over several centuries. This shift began with the Muslim conquest in the seventh century CE, when Muslim Arab forces conquered the region from the Byzantine and Sasanian Empires between 636-651 CE, under the Rashidun Caliphate. This marked the initial Muslim takeover of the area.

Christianity was the dominant religion in Mesopotamia during the early Islamic period from the seventh to eleventh centuries. The Church of the East and the Christian community had a strong presence during this time. However, the Christian population began to decline due to factors like heavy taxation, social discrimination, and gradual conversions to Islam.

The Seljuk Turks conquered Mesopotamia in the eleventh

century, further marginalizing the remaining Christian communities. By the thirteenth century, Islam had become the majority religion in the region. Under the Mongol and then the Ottoman empires, the Christian populations in Mesopotamia continued to dwindle. However, some Christian communities managed to persist, like the Chaldean Catholic Church. By the sixteenth century, Mesopotamia was firmly under Ottoman Muslim rule, and the Christian population had become a small minority. This demographic shift solidified in the centuries that followed, up until the present day.

"And get this—for centuries, the Tomb of Columbus himself was housed right here. Can you imagine? Of course, that was long after my time, but a guy can still appreciate a bit of history, you know?"

Victor explained that because Columbus died in Seville, Spain, he was initially buried there. But his wish was to be buried in Santa Maria la Menor. So when the church was built, his son Diego ordered the transfer of his remains from Seville to Santo Domingo. Then, the Spaniards decided to move his remains back to Seville in 1795, to save them from the French who had won the land in their Revolutionary Wars.

"Some people say his bones are in Havana, some say in the Columbus lighthouse nearby, don't believe it," said Victor. "It's all fake news."

That term was completely foreign to Elias, but he didn't ask any questions.

Chapter 12

Elias' Journey from Piura to Trujillo

After spending ten days in Piura, Elias left, heading for a village called Lilmoa. He proceeded along a barren track lacking in water, and as sandy as the land of Egypt. All the inhabitants of this village were Indians, with only their bishop being Spanish. Some were true Christians, while the rest were Christian out of fear.

The indigenous peoples Elias encountered in the Andes region, such as the Inca, practiced complex polytheistic religions prior to the arrival of the Spanish. The Inca civilization had a rich cosmology centered around the worship of creator gods like Viracocha, as well as sacred mountains, rivers, and celestial bodies. These traditional beliefs were deeply woven into the Andean communities' ways of life and relationship with the natural world.

However, as the Spanish conquistadors colonized the Andes, they sought to impose Christianity and Catholicism on the indigenous populations through a combination of religious preaching and political/military force. Missionaries worked to convert Andean people, while the Spanish colonial authorities used coercion and violence to suppressing traditional spiritual practices. As evidenced by Elias' account, some indigenous people outwardly adopted Christianity "out of fear," while maintaining their ancestral beliefs privately. Others resolutely resisted conversion, as seen in the village where "only their bishop is Spanish." This disruption of indigenous religious traditions significantly impacted the Andean cosmological worldview that had thrived for centuries before the Spanish conquest.

This once again reminded Elias of his birthland Mesopotamia, where the Ottoman Empire had similarly imposed Islam and their way of life on the region's Christian populations. Like the Andean peoples, many Christians in Mesopotamia may have appeared to convert outwardly under Ottoman rule but continued to practice their faith secretly. Both colonized groups displayed remarkable resilience in maintaining elements of their ancestral spiritual connections, even in the face of attempts to eradicate them.

Over centuries, the religious landscapes of both the Andes and Mesopotamia became characterized by vibrant syncretism. Indigenous deities, spirits, and sacred sites continued to be revered alongside Christian saints and rituals. This multicultural religious tapestry reflects the adaptive capacity of Andean and Mesopotamian communities to preserve their spiritual heritage, blending traditional and Abrahamic elements into unique hybrid cultures.

"Today, the Andes is home to these vibrant, hybrid religious cultures that retain pre-Columbian indigenous influences alongside Catholic and Christian traditions," Victor said as he walked alongside Elias. He stopped and looked at Elias. "Your people will one day come to the Americas and they will compare themselves to the natives who were colonized."

The next day, Elias left for an Indian town called Lombayeque. This town was large, inhabited by rich Indians and some Spaniards. The bishop's deputy invited Elias to his home and asked him to hold mass on Sunday, addressing the Indians in Spanish. Elias conducted mass as requested, speaking to a congregation of thirty-five priests and around three thousand commoners. They were greatly pleased with his sermon, admiring his long beard and the ornate papal robe he had been gifted by the Pope. The robe was a traditional Eastern-rite vestment, adorned with the Pope's personal insignia and medallion. All the parishioners sought Elias' blessing, as he had brought them gifts of rosaries and crosses from Jerusalem.

Five days later, Elias left and headed for a town called Sagna (or Zana). This town was large, inhabited by both Indians and Spaniards, with a large river flowing next to it. Elias often traveled by night, riding in a litter or "tahtiravan" to avoid the intense heat. One night, the muleteer dozed off, and the mules strayed from the path, entering a vast, endless forest. Elias ordered his servants to dismount and wait, so they would not stray further and perish, as had happened to others. In the morning, Elias had the muleteer light a large fire and smoke to signal their location. Their companions had gone ahead and realized Elias' party was running late, so they dispatched a search party. This search party located them by spotting a white banner that Elias had the muleteer place in a tall tree.

The forest was predominantly composed of wild white cotton trees, belonging to no single owner. The cotton plants had a coarse rough texture, akin to that of a pomegranate. Their fruits were small yet robust, and the cotton fibers themselves were long and woolly in nature. The local indigenous people freely gathered this cotton to weave into skirts and other essential textiles. This communally accessible resource was invaluable, allowing the Andean communities to fulfill their clothing needs through traditional weaving practices. The resilient, renewable cotton forest provided a sustainable supply of this vital raw material.

Two days later, Elias reached the town, which was inhabited by Spaniards and Indians and governed by a general. Elias remained there for four days, enjoying the hospitality of the general and the bishop's deputy. From there, he left for Trujillo, traveling for ten days along a difficult road with few rest stops and scarce provisions. Elias had brought his own food and a spare horse. When the weather turned cool, he would ride one horse, and when the animal grew tired, he rode the other.

The large town of Trujillo had monks and nuns belonging to the order of St. Francis and the Jesuit, also bishops and some two thousand priests. Their bishop had recently died and his position vacant. The Franciscan monks invited Elias to conduct mass on the feast of St. Francis, October 4th. Elias, wearing the ornate papal robe gifted to him, had the Pope's medallion and signet drawn upon it, greatly impressing the people in the full church. Many sought the blessing from it.

Elias spent ten days in this town, then set out once more, this time seeking the town of Cajamarca.

Chapter 13

Elias' Journey to Lima

Situated atop a mountain, Cajamarca was inhabited by a powerful indigenous ruler known as the Inca, or "Incarasuf" as Elias referred to him. Elias remained in Cajamarca for three days, during which time Victor showed up and with a somber expression, told him of the tragic tale of the last Inca emperor, Atahualpa.

Victor started by saying, "On July 26th, 1533, in the late afternoon. Atahualpa, the final Sapa Inca, was brought to the public square of Cajamarca, a city in the Andean highlands, which is now northern Peru." He paused, his gaze meeting Elias's. "His captors, the Spanish conquistadors led by Francisco Pizarro, had just made the fateful decision that Atahualpa must die."

Elias nodded solemnly, his eyes reflecting the weight of history being shared.

"During the nine months of his captivity," Victor continued, "those Spaniards who had dealings with the emperor were impressed by him. They described him as 'good looking... with a fine face, handsome and fierce.' They admired his dignity, his reason, and his good humor, knowing him to be a wise man."

Nodding thoughtfully, Elias stroked his beard.

"But there were rumors of a massive Inca army, 200,000 strong, coming to free their beloved ruler," Victor recounted.

Pizarro challenged Atahualpa, who replied, "What am I, and all my people, that we should trouble such valiant men as you are?" Victor shook his head sadly. "Unsure, Pizarro ordered the emperor to be chained by the neck. But the Spanish were still gripped by fear. Death, it seemed, was the only answer."

Elias let out a heavy sigh, the parallels to his own people's struggles under Ottoman rule not lost on him.

"The first plan was to burn Atahualpa as a heretic, tying him to a stake," Victor continued. "But when he agreed to convert to Christianity, he was instead strangled. His body was then left in the public square for all to see."

Victor's gaze locked with Elias's, a deep sorrow reflected in his eyes. "It is said that Atahualpa wept when he realized his fate. Even Pizarro, it is written, was unable to spare the emperor's life and wept as well."

The two men stood in somber silence, the weight of this tragic history hanging in the air between them.

"There are certainly parallels to be drawn, my friend," Elias said. "The Inca Empire, like the Chaldean, was a vast and formidable civilization—until the arrival of foreign conquerors who sought to subjugate and reshape it to their will."

He paused, a hint of sadness in his voice.

"Like Atahualpa, my people have also faced ruthless ambitions that aim to extinguish our traditions and way of life," Elias said.

Victor nodded solemnly, his expression somber. "A tragic fate, indeed. But perhaps there is some solace in knowing that the spirit and legacy of the Inca lives on, even if their empire fell. Isn't that the case with Chaldeans too?"

Elias offered a smile, his eyes brightening. "The resilience of human civilization, no matter the challenges, is truly remarkable."

Victor clasped Elias on the shoulder, a warm smile

spreading across his face. "Well said, my friend. Now, shall we continue our journey through this remarkable history? There is much more to discover about the Inca and their enduring influence on this land."

Elias nodded, and the two men set off, their footsteps echoing across the ancient ruins.

On the fourth day, Elias departed Cajamarca and made his way towards the town of Lima, where the Spanish colonial governor, or "minister of the king," resided and governed the region. Descending the mountain, Elias reached a formidable river called the Santa, which had no crossing point. The local indigenous people created a clever solution using dried gourds and wooden planks. They made a raft or "balsa" to transport people and goods across dangerous waters. The animals, meanwhile, had to brave the strong currents by swimming.

Elias and his companions, including two men, one wounded in battle and the other bitten by a snake, crossed the Santa River cautiously, seeking divine protection. From there, they continued their journey, passing through lands abundant with sugarcane plantations and textile factories, evidence of the Spanish colonial economy's grip on the region.

After an eight-day journey, Elias arrived in the bustling colonial city of Lima. Upon reaching his destination, he first alighted at the home of the Inquisitor, who was an old acquaintance from Spain. Elias had previously loaned the Inquisitor 1,400 piasters in the city of Portobelo, Panama, and had profited handsomely from the interest payments.

Elias, feeling refreshed from his travels, then sought an audience with the colonial governor, Don Balthasar Villagucunda de Castillar, Marquis of Aragon. He presented the royal decree and letters of recommendation he had brought from Spain. The governor, one of the Spanish nobility's most esteemed representatives in the New World, warmly received Elias and promised to assist him in any way he could.

Elias also visited the governor's wife, who likewise welcomed him with great honor. The couple, though married for fourteen years, had no children. Next, Elias paid his respects to the local clergy, including the archdeacon and other priests gathered for prayer in the church. The bishopric of Lima, with an annual income of 50,000 piasters and oversight of 120 priests, was currently vacant, as the previous bishop had recently passed away. The faithful were awaiting the arrival of a new bishop from Spain.

During his stay in Lima, Elias fell gravely ill, but the governor's personal physicians attended to him. He recovered after twenty days, giving credit to the Virgin Mary. The governor, who had sent his treasurer with loads of sweets twice a day to check on Elias during his illness, joyfully received him upon his return to health. At that moment, Elias witnessed a failed demonstration by a mine owner who claimed to have discovered a new, mercury-free technique for extracting silver. When they researched the technique, they found it to be a false invention.

Once Elias was well, Victor reappeared, like a genie from a bottle. He congratulated Elias on his recovery and offered to give him insights about the culture and beliefs of the people in Peru before the Spanish colonization. Elias accepted.

Victor explained that before the arrival of the Spaniards, the locals worshipped idols and celestial bodies. They had no knowledge of crafts, reading, or writing. He also mentioned that they were renowned for their advanced agricultural practices, pottery, and textiles.

"So how do they view the Spanish colonization?" Elias asked.

"Colonialism involves a country seizing control of another, denying self-governance, exploiting resources, and using force," Victor clarified. Colonialism in the Americas led to the deaths of millions of native people. The European conquerors killed many, and diseases brought over from Europe caused additional deaths due to the lack of immunity among the locals. It is worth mentioning that the Inca population had already been exposed to diseases prior to the Spanish arrival. In Mexico, the Spanish had settled for months before plagues started affecting the Aztecs. This had catastrophic effects on both empires. Regardless, it was all very bad!"

He stopped and looked sternly at Elias. "But colonization has ancient roots, with examples dating back over five thousand years. The earliest known instances include the Sumerians and Akkadians in Mesopotamia, the Phoenicians around 1200 BCE, and the Greek city-states in the eighth century BCE."

Elias nodded, reflecting and pulling gently at his beard.

"Before the Spaniards arrived to the Americas, it was common practice for natives to make war on native tribes and take, or colonize, if you will, their hunting lands. This made them different than the Europeans in two ways; they were here first and this time, they were the colonized."

Listening to Victor, Elias thought that Europeans were really no different than every other major culture who practiced colonization. He told Victor this and Victor said, "Even when it comes to slavery, they are no different."

He went on to explain that the Egyptian pyramids, for instance, were built by slaves. Brazil imported more African slaves than any other country, with over four million slaves brought to Brazil between the sixteenth and nineteenth centuries. Many Caribbean islands, including Cuba, Jamaica, Barbados, and Haiti, had economies heavily reliant on slave labor, especially in the production of sugar, tobacco, and other cash crops. The European colonial powers, namely Spain, Portugal, the Netherlands, and the United Kingdom, relied on forced African labor in the Americas, the Caribbean, and other regions to develop their overseas empires and economies. Slavery existed in parts of the Middle East and North Africa for centuries and was used to produce agricultural goods and provide domestic labor. Countries like Saudi Arabia, Yemen, and Oman had significant slave populations. Even within Africa, there were local slave trades and slavery systems operating, often fueled by wars and the sale of captives to European and Arab slave traders. Yet it was the Caucasian nations that were the first to outlaw slavery.

"And slavery is still a very prevalent practice in Africa," said Victor.

"Tell me about the other indigenous tribes in the Americas," Elias said as they walked.

Victor began with a wry smile, "The Mayans, bless their hearts, had their heyday about a thousand years before the Spanish showed up. But then their society just went and collapsed, shifting away from those fancy inland cities to the ones further up the peninsula." He shrugged. "Now, the reasons for that are up for debate, but one possibility is that good ol' ecological collapse—you know, too much land clearing." Victor chuckled and continued, "But hey, the Mayans were like the cool kids on the block back then. They were the cultural contemporaries and successors to the Olmec, who really set the tone for a lot of those major Mesoamerican civilizations. You know, the core deities, the origin myths, the ball game—the whole nine yards."

His expression turned more serious as he discussed the

Mayans' practices. "Now, the Mayans, they did dabble in a little human sacrifice here and there. But let's be real, so did a lot of the other groups—the Incas, Zapotec, Mixtec, Teotihuacan, and the like. It was usually for special occasions, you know, like when they were finishing up a new temple or crowning a new ruler. Heck, even the solstice and equinox got the sacrificial treatment sometimes." He paused, then added with bit of disgust, "But the Aztecs, they just went fucking nuts with it."

"How is that?" asked Elias.

"They ruled over vast empire with an iron fist, butchered local tribes who sought independence or attempted to assert their autonomy. In his letters to the King of Spain, Hernan Cortes described the indigenous peoples' brutality, as if he'd walked into a Satanic horror movie where Aztec priests ritually extracted the hearts of sacrifice victims, flaying young girls alive to wear their skins, and offering tens of thousands of sacrifices to their deities."

"Victor, what are horror movies?" Elias asked.

"Ahh, that's ahead of your time, Padre," Victor said, adding, "I mean, it wasn't for nothing that the American Declaration of Independence called them 'merciless Indian savages.'"

"But the Europeans were violent too," said Elias.

"Yes, they were, but not to the extent as the Aztecs."

Elias nodded and Victor went on to discuss the burial customs of the indigenous people. For Indian deaths, a tomb of about two meters high and three long was used. The tools of his profession were placed in the tomb with him, with one gulf of corn wine. Corn wine, or chicha, was a fermented beverage made from maize that was commonly consumed in pre-Columbian Andean cultures. Placing corn wine in tombs likely served as a ritual or offering for the deceased, nourishing them in the afterlife.

"What were the similarities and differences between the Aztecs and Incas?" Elias asked, finding the burial information a bit boring.

"Well Padre, as we explore these remarkable civilizations," Victor began. "Let's start with their similarities. Both the Inca and Aztec empires were incredibly powerful, conquering hundreds of cities that often resented their rule and heavy taxation. Sadly, both empires met their end due to Spanish invasions. The Spanish took advantage of existing divisions, introduced devastating diseases, and employed advanced technology like guns, horses, and steel."

As they walked past a display of ancient artifacts, Victor pointed out, "Both civilizations shared a belief in multiple gods, or polytheism. Agriculture played a vital role too; the Incas were adept at farming potatoes, while the Aztecs relied heavily on corn. Both societies were built on the backbone of their agricultural achievements."

He continued, "Now, what were their differences, you ask, aside from one going berserk with human sacrifices versus the other going easy on it? Well, the Incas were in the Bronze Age, showcasing advanced metallurgy, while the Aztecs operated in the Stone Age. Interestingly, the Aztecs developed a system of writing, while the Incas used Quipu—a series of knotted strings—for record-keeping."

He explained that the governance systems also varied. The Incas had a more centralized approach, assigning governors and relocating conquered peoples to maintain control. In contrast, the Aztecs functioned as a tributary empire, with many rivals still left unconquered.

The Inca military, like the Romans, depended on seasoned units and officers. They employed various weapons like bronze axes, bows and arrows, spears, and slings for casting stones. On the other hand, the Aztecs had a feudalistic structure. They were divided into elite knights and commoners. Their weapons included obsidian blades, arrowheads, and spear points, which they heavily relied on.

Victor mentioned that the Incas did not have horses, mules, donkeys, oxen, cows, sheep, or even chicken. "The Incas used llamas, which look like camels, for transport and their sophisticated courier system with Chasquis along well-maintained roads. Llamas could not travel longer than twelve miles, and when tired, they slept, foamed at the mouth, and spat at its owner.

Education was another point of divergence. While the Incas allowed women into their schools, they excluded commoners. Conversely, the Aztecs prohibited women from education but allowed peasant men to learn.

As the tour wrapped up, Victor concluded with one last reflection. "Before we finish, let's consider the political struggles that led to the downfalls of these empires. The Inca Empire faced a significant political crisis characterized by a civil war between two brothers, Atahualpa and Huáscar. This internal conflict weakened their unity at a crucial time. The Aztec Empire faced challenges in a three-way power struggle among the King, the Priests, the Aristocracy, and the military. This complex power dynamic created divisions that ultimately contributed to their vulnerability during the Spanish conquest."

After that intense guided tour with Victor, Elias decided to continued the rest of the trip in the bustling city of Lima on his own. The city's landscape, he learned, was marked by the ever-present threat of natural disasters. It was frequently shaken by severe earthquakes, a testament to the region's dynamic geological history. Despite the challenges of the environment, Elias found solace in the warm reception from the city's governor. The governor had instructed the wider region to extend their hospitality to the weary traveler.

Elias' time in Lima was further enriched by the city's vibrant religious landscape. The grand cathedral, serving as the bishopric's seat, was the heart of this spiritual tapestry and a testament to the enduring presence of the Catholic faith in the region. Surrounding the cathedral was a tapestry of monasteries and churches, each representing a different religious order: the Franciscans, Augustinians, Jesuits, and the brothers of Mercy, to name a few. These institutions not only provided Elias with a sense of community, but also extended to him the privilege of celebrating mass within their hallowed walls.

One experience stood out for him. His stay in the city was marked by invitations to hold mass in the churches and monasteries. The local clergy extended warm hospitality and consideration to him. Don Juan Batista de la Cantera, a pious man, provided refuge for Elias when he fell ill. During his recovery, Don Juan made sure that Elias had everything he needed, further solidifying their gesture.

Elias' time in Lima was not without its challenges, however. The city was expensive, with a single chicken costing one and a half piasters. Yet even this obstacle was overcome through the generosity of the local ecclesiastical community. Upon Elias' recovery, the "Cabildo" chapter of the priesthood organized a grand procession to visit him. They escorted him to the church and bestowed him with the honor of sitting beside the archdeacon, the second-highest position after the bishop. Elias was then invited to hold mass. He did so in the

Chaldean language, that is, Eastern Syriac, which delighted the congregation.

The outpouring of support from the religious institutions of Lima did not stop there. After Elias' mass, the Cabildo convened and presented him with a sum of one thousand piasters, a remarkable display of financial support. Other religious institutions also joined in, presenting Elias with numerous gifts and providing him with a carriage, four mules, and a black slave attendant for his stay.

Chapter 14

The Journey to Huancavelica

At the end of the year, Elias approached the colonial governor in Lima. He asked for permission to explore the legendary Andean mountains, which were said to hold vast treasures of silver and gold. Recognizing Elias' scholarly curiosity and distinguished reputation, the governor readily granted the request. The governor, eager to help the young scholar, wrote letters of introduction to regional administrators and church authorities. In these letters, he instructed them to provide Elias with utmost hospitality during his travels.

The governor also assigned one of his most seasoned military officers to accompany Elias as a guide and facilitator. This seasoned soldier would travel ahead, making all the necessary logistical arrangements—securing food, lodging, and other provisions, often by calling upon the hospitality of local village headmen. With this experienced military escort in tow, Elias set out from Lima, his sights set on the remote town of Huancavelica.

For the first two days, the journey proceeded smoothly along a well-trodden path. But on the third day, they began to ascend a formidable, snow-capped mountain, where the winds grew bitterly cold and the climate radically shifted. Elias and his companion found their moods and dispositions changing as they abruptly transitioned from the sweltering heat of the coastal lowlands to the frigid mountain air.

Reaching the mountain's peak, they arrived at a place ominously known as *Bonada Bariacaca*, "the roar of drunkenness." This remote spot was linked to indigenous rituals and revelry for a long time. It harkens back to the pre-Columbian era when the Inca Empire extracted mineral wealth from the surrounding mountains, including legendary silver and mercury deposits.

As they pressed onward, Elias and his guide encountered the Provincial, the regional head of the Franciscan order. The Provincial inquired about their journey, and Elias described the jarring climatic shifts they had endured. The Provincial then parted ways, taking a different road.

The next obstacle was crossing the turbulent waters of the River Boni. A rickety bridge, woven from hemp ropes and tied precariously to trees on either bank, spanned the raging torrent. With great caution, they led their mounts across this perilous crossing.

Finally, ten days after setting out, they reached the remote town of Huancavelica—a small, isolated settlement dominated by the imposing presence of a massive mercury-stone mine. Elias took up residence in the local Jesuit compound. He observed the shifting winds in this high-altitude town, which changed three times a day. Additionally, he noted how the late afternoon rains contributed to the settlement's notoriously unhealthy climate.

One day, Elias ventured out to inspect the mercury mines in the district, accompanied by the governor. He was impressed by what he saw—the workers cutting stones from the mine and extracting the mercury within. They showed him the process in detail. First, they placed the stones containing mercury in a building with a perforated floor, lining it with rows of brass containers. Wood stacked atop stones, heated to high temperatures. As the stones heated, the mercury would vaporize and drip down into the containers below. After a day and night of controlled temperature changes, they removed the stones and ashes and collected the pure mercury from the containers.

Elias noticed a deputy of the king on site, managing production for the monarch. This deputy would compensate the mine owners at a rate of fifty-two piasters per quintal (a unit of measure equal to about a hundred pounds). The deputy's task was to sell the mercury to silver mine owners at ninety piasters per quintal. This was because the owners used the mercury in the process of extracting silver from ore.

Seizing the chance to bless the miners and operations, he held mass at the mine's central altar. The mine owners offered him a "bashkash"—a gift—of fifty quintals of mercury, requesting he wait a month for it to be extracted. However, Elias had to decline, as the king of Spain had decreed a strict ban on the sale of mercury, with severe penalties for any violations.

The mercury mines of South America, like the one Elias visited, had a long and storied history. Rev. Feuillée, a French nuncio to Peru during the same time as Elias, gave a thorough account of these mines. He described how they were extensively excavated into a vast mountain near Huancavelica and contained multiple residential and worship areas within the mining complex. He told him about the Santa Barbara Mine, discovered in 1571, which played a key role in Peru's silver exploitation. It is often referred to as "the mine of death" due to its harsh conditions.

Elias encountered a remarkable natural phenomenon in this particular town—a type of "petrified water." This brownish-colored liquid, when poured into containers and left exposed to the air for eight days, would solidify and turn to stone. The locals used this unique material to construct their homes. He witnessed this process firsthand and even got to see an intriguing experiment. If wood sits in water for forty days, the submerged part turns to stone, but the exposed part remains wood. Someone showed Elias a demonstration of a cross made from a composite of petrified wood and stone.

Rev. Feuillée had documented before this phenomenon of "petrified water". The water found by Feuillée came out of the ground very hot and solidified quickly upon contact with air. This allowed the locals to mold and shape it into desired forms and structures.

After observing this marvel, Elias departed the town ten days later, accompanied by fourteen men who had come to bid him farewell. He then continued on the path leading to a town called Aguamanga, passing through a landscape filled with a distinctive type of tree known as the "tocal" or "tunal."

These trees, with their thick, thorn-covered leaves and absence of branches, bore a fruit called "tuna" in the local language. The tuna fruit, smaller than a chicken egg but significantly harder, had a sweet and refreshing interior. However, its exterior was covered in soft spines, which made handling it a delicate task. The entire countryside and surrounding mountains were teeming with these peculiar, cactus-like plants commonly found in the Near East, especially along coastal regions.

The prevalence of this hardy plant suggests a drier climate in the region Elias was traveling through, which is different from the one he was accustomed to back home. The tuna fruit's combination of protective spines and sweet, nourishing flesh would have made it an important food source for the local population in this rugged, desert-like environment.

Chapter 15

The Town of Aguamanga

After several days of arduous travel, Elias arrived in the town of Aguamanga. The Jesuit residence there was to be his lodging, as the head Jesuit had sent letters instructing his subordinates to provide Elias with shelter. This town has a rich history, being the former seat of a wealthy bishop who was also the first head of the local Inquisition. His name was Don Christofolo de Castello, and he had wielded significant influence in the region during his tenure.

The next morning, two priests came on behalf of the current bishop to welcome Elias and congratulate him on his arrival. Eager to meet the local dignitary, Elias visited the bishop's residence early that same day. The bishop himself rose to greet Elias warmly, inquiring about his background and experiences. Impressed by Elias, the bishop invited him to partake in a luncheon at his estate later that afternoon.

Delighted by the bishop's hospitality, Elias gladly accepted the invitation. Following a pleasant meal, the bishop presented Elias with an exquisite golden chain worth two hundred piasters—a lavish gesture that did not go unnoticed by the notables of Aguamanga. Word of the bishop's honor bestowed upon Elias quickly spread, and soon a steady stream of the town's prominent citizens arrived to pay their respects and meet the esteemed guest.

Eager to return the hospitality, four days later Elias accompanied two Jesuit priests on a tour of the town's many rich churches and monasteries. The bishop arranged for local companions to take Elias to the homes of those who had called on him. The Jesuits had written their names one by one.

Victor appeared at Elias' door with a grin after eight days of exploring religious sites and resting. It was a beautiful morning as the sun rose over the Andes, casting a golden hue on the landscape. "Welcome to Aguamanga, my friend! Ready to explore some hidden gems?"

"Sure, but I've already visited several religious sites…"

"Come on," Victor interrupted, enthusiastically, lead the way. "Let's kick things off at the Aguamanga Thermal Baths. These hot springs are not just a place to relax, they're a slice of paradise. Legend has it that the Incas believed these waters had healing powers. I mean, who wouldn't want to soak in a bit of ancient magic?"

As they arrived at the thermal baths, steam rose gently from the water, creating an inviting atmosphere. "Look at that," Victor said, gesturing with a flourish. "Now, that's what I call a natural spa! Just remember, it's not a race; it's about enjoying the moment."

After a refreshing dip, they continued their journey to the Inca Ruins. "These structures are like the whispers of history," Victor remarked, examining the stonework. "They tell tales of a civilization that thrived long before our time. Can you imagine the stories these walls could tell?"

Elias looked around.

"And speaking of civilization, let's not forget about the stunning landscapes here. This area is perfect for hiking." Victor looked at Elias' feet. "Padre, are your shoes comfortable enough for the tasks?"

Elias nodded.

As they made their way to a local market, Victor said, "And now, for the grand finale: the local markets! This is where you can find everything from handmade textiles to delicious local snacks. I recommend trying the empanadas. They're like a hug for your stomach!"

With laughter echoing in the air, they continued their exploration, each step uncovering more of Aguamanga's charm.

Back at home, the bishop decreed that a special play be performed in Elias' honor. The play dramatized the life of the Roman saint known as San Alexius, or Mâr Rîsha in Arabic. It depicted the saint's deeds, including how he gave his bride a ring before departing to wander the world. Elias, along with the enthusiastic townspeople, thoroughly enjoyed the performance. Elias had a powerful ally in the governor, so the people of Aguamanga made great efforts to ensure his stay was comfortable and memorable. Elias ended up remaining in the town for a total of twenty days, basking in the hospitality and honors bestowed upon him.

Elias then prepared to leave for the city of Cuzo. The governor, the head of the Jesuit order, and friends came to say goodbye before his departure. They traveled together for about half a parsang before saying their goodbyes and parting ways, with the others returning to town while Elias continued his journey.

Chapter 16

Cuzco, Peru

Two days later, Elias and his party reached the Apurimac River. This formidable river, named for the Quechua words "apu" meaning "lord" and "rimaq" meaning "speaker", had long been an important landmark in the region. The Inca had constructed an impressive woven bridge made from tree roots and branches to span its width, around a yard wide and twenty yards long. Crossing the bridge was dangerous. The Indians had to unload the mules and carry the cargo across one by one on their backs. They stripped the mules of their gear and carefully led them across the swaying structure described by Elias as "shaking like a cradle when rocked by someone's foot." If a mule's leg slips through the boards, the Indians must free the edges and let the animal fall into the river rapids, relying on its swimming ability to cross.

Elias and his companions crossed the bridge with great trepidation, thankful to reach the far side safely. As they pressed on, they encountered a variety of wildlife native to the desolate Andean mountains, including horses, wild llamas, mules, donkeys, and a particular creature called the vicuña. This camelid relative of the llama resembled a graceful, hornless gazelle, and was known for its friendly temperament and exceptionally soft, fine wool, prized by the local indigenous people. Elias hunted and killed some vicuñas, but only the Indians ate them. Within the stomach of the vicuña, a valuable bezoar stone could sometimes be found, long prized as a powerful antidote to poisons.

The bezoar stone, known also as hazahr in Persian, meaning "antidote", was a substance long prized by Arab doctors for its purported ability to counteract poisons. Its reputation grew even more intense as it reached the Western lands, where it was called Bezuar in Portuguese and Bezoard in French.

According to the Arab author al-Tifashi, there were two main types of bezoar stones—one animal-derived and the other mineral. Al-Tifashi reported that the mineral variety of bezoar stones could be found in abundance between the Isle of Ibn 'Umar and Mosul in Iraq. These stones were large, soft, and would turn white when rubbed. As for the animal-derived bezoar, the focus of his discussion was a light yellowish stone with a layered, dotted appearance that dissolved rapidly with friction, also turning white. Chinese sources typically imported these stones to the region, weighing between one-eighth and one-half ounce.

Interestingly, al-Tifashi observed that the bezoar was found in the "cattle" (likely referring to camelids) of Peru as well. He also mentioned that the Persian root of the word, "pak zahr", meant "that which cleanses the body of poison." People believed the stone expelled toxins from veins and saved the afflicted from death. In earlier centuries, it was a potent medicine, but its legitimacy remained unverified.

Three days later, Elias and his companions entered a vast sugarcane plantation known as Abancay. This expansive land belonged to the Jesuit order, who oversaw the yearly harvest of 30,000 khandicary—an imperial Persian unit of measure—of sugar. Slaves carried the backbreaking labor of plowing the fields and making sugar.

After traversing the plantation, Elias and his party reached the town of Abancay itself three days later. This settlement had once been the domain of the Inca king Atahualpa, brother of the previous ruler Huáscar. As he approached the town, the Jesuits, who escorted him to their monastery, greeted with great fanfare him. This opulent complex had once been the very palace of the Inca king, its vast gardens and convent taking up half the size of the town. Elias marveled at the intricate stonework, carved by the ancient Inca without the aid of iron tools, yet displaying remarkable symmetry.

The town itself was a vibrant mix of Spanish and indigenous inhabitants, numbering four thousand and three thousand households, respectively. Spanish children had schools, and the Jesuits built one for Indian children.

The bishop and the Jesuit priests, who fought over the honor of hosting him, received Elias with great hospitality. Even the governor, an old traveling companion from Spain, insisted that Elias stay with him, though Elias declined these invitations.

The following day, the esteemed bishop of the town came to visit Elias. Soon after, the rest of the notable figures and monastery leaders of the community also paid their respects to the distinguished traveler. Several days later, Elias returned these visits, accompanied by two Jesuit priests. Together they rode out in Elias's carriage to call upon the bishop and other prominent members of the local society.

When Elias arrived in the town of Abancay, the local bishop, clergy, and prominent citizens immediately requested that he preside over mass in the grand church. Elias gladly obliged, conducting the service in the Eastern Syriac liturgical language.

The overseer in the town invited Elias to celebrate mass, and he had two archdeacons to assist him. Elias was generously and respectfully received by all, with the convents and other institutions offering him valuable gifts.

The cathedral's council of canons also presented Elias with a befitting present, and the bishop of Abancay himself sent Elias a gift to match. Some local friends further offered Elias the use of a carriage to explore the monuments of the ancient Inca outside the town.

Among the remarkable sites Elias witnessed were the tombs of the Inca rulers of old. Rows of elaborate structures, standing roughly two yards high, one and a half yards wide, and three yards long, adorned the earth's surface. The Incas believed their rulers were sons of the sun god Inti and practiced mummification after death. This involved removing the organs, preserving the body with alcohol, and utilizing the cold, dry mountain air to freeze their remains. Similar to ancient Egyptian pharaohs, these royal mummies were buried with treasures and offerings to accompany them in the afterlife. Many of these elaborate tombs can be found near Ñaupa Iglesia outside Abancay, where the remains of influential Inca leaders lie in honor of their significance.

Elias also learned of a dramatic natural disaster that had recently struck the region. An earthquake outside the town, about two parasangs away, had caused a mountain bordering a river to collapse into the water, blocking its flow. The resulting flood had devastated nearby plantations and three entire villages. The seismic event reached Lima, causing damage and panic among the inhabitants. Such seismic events are not uncommon in Peru, which is situated along the Pacific Ring of Fire.

Elias ended up staying in the town of Cuzco for five months, delayed by the onset of winter and the resulting impassibility of the swollen rivers. During this extended sojourn, he continued to be hosted with the utmost hospitality by the local community.

Chapter 17

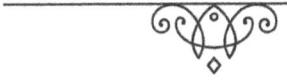

Coca

Elias left Cuzco when the time was up, heading towards Paucartambo. He arrived after six days of travel, staying in various settlements each night. Upon entering Paucartambo, a welcoming party of Dominican friars and the local governor, who escorted him into the town, greeted Elias. Elias was hosted at the governor's residence, as the official was an attendant of the viceroy, Elias's esteemed friend.

Victor visited Elias' dwelling and expressed his desire to show him around Paucartambo. The town served as a frontier between Spanish settlements and the lands of the pagan indigenous tribes. These native groups raided the Spanish communities, capturing men, women, and children to enslave. The indigenous people would sometimes even slaughter, barbecue, and eat Spanish captives, holding ceremonial feasts.

"Really?" Elias asked, curiosity evident in his voice.

"Yes, that's documented in several historical accounts such as the chroniclers of Bernal Díaz del Castillo mentioned the brutal treatment of captives during the conquests."

"What else do these sources say?" Elias asked, leaning in.

"Well," Victor continued, "some indigenous groups saw this as a way to assert power and resist colonization. Fray Bartolomé de las Casas also wrote about these practices, highlighting the violent clashes and the complex relationships between the Spanish and the natives."

"That's fascinating and quite brutal," Elias remarked, shaking his head. "It really shows the harsh realities of that time."

"Absolutely," Victor agreed. "It's important to understand the context and the perspectives of both sides during these encounters."

The native inhabitants of the region, Victor told Elias, chewed a certain type of grass called coca. It had intoxicating effects, akin to drinking wine. "An inhabitant of the suburbs of Cuzco might refrain from food but not from chewing the grass of coca because in it he finds food, drink and medicine," he said.

"Was this grass an early form of the drug cocaine?" Elias asked.

"Not exactly," Victor replied. "Coca leaves are really important in Andean culture. People chew them for energy and to help with hunger. They also have medicinal benefits, like treating altitude sickness. It's key to remember that coca leaves are natural and used in everyday life, while processed cocaine is a whole different thing."

"I heard they have no wheat or barley, only Egyptian corn, from which they make an alcoholic drink that makes them drunk."

"That's true," Victor replied. "The indigenous people here brew an alcoholic drink that's similar to the Middle Eastern spirit called arak, which, as you know, is made from grapes or dates."

"Sounds like they had their own strong traditions," Elias noted.

"They did. These tribes were great in number and physically formidable, living in the high mountains and led by powerful chieftains. The Spanish settlers found it hard to resist their strength and raiding tactics."

Chapter 18

Cruel Death of a Silver Miner

Elias embarked on a journey to the silver mine of Condoruma. However, the harsh cold and strong winds of the Andes limited his stay to just three days. He then traveled to Cailloma, where he observed indigenous workers extracting silver. They ground stones into a fine powder, mixed it with mercury, and stirred the mixture for ten to twelve days to bind the silver particles. Afterward, they washed the mixture to separate the silver from the dirt. Elias proceeded to the village of Lampa. There, he observed indigenous people building a church, guided by a wealthy Spanish priest who had invested 200,000 pieces of eight in its construction.

Elias felt sadness as he witnessed how greed caused the cruel death of a wealthy man from Seville. His name was Don Jose Salcedo, and he held dominion over the renowned Bono mine. A man of unbridled success, paid a staggering 2,700,000 piasters in taxes to the king on the silver extracted from his mine. He could reportedly gather an impressive 6,000 piasters worth of silver daily from the mine.

However, Salcedo's prosperity and generosity earned him the envy of certain individuals. His detractors conspired against him, devising a plot to accuse him of conspiring with "white folk" to seize control of the town. Swiftly relayed false allegations reached the governor, who wasted no time responding.

The governor descended upon the Mines of Bono, where Salcedo lived, and promptly arrested him. They then took the unfortunate man to Lima. The governor hung some of Salcedo's trusted companions and confiscated their wealth, along with the Bono mine itself, in the king's name. The governor also confiscated the 10,000 quintals of silver ore that the mine had extracted.

Salcedo, now imprisoned, pleaded with the governor, imploring him to present his case before the king of Spain. He offered a simple request: "If the king orders my death, then kill me; and if he orders my release, then set me free, and I will honor all my commitments while held in your prison." But the governor and his council, driven by greed, refused to heed Salcedo's pleas and swiftly decreed his execution.

The news of Salcedo's unjust fate swiftly spread, rallying the people of neighboring towns and villages—the poor, monks, nuns, orphans, and widows—to collectively pray and implore God for Salcedo's liberation. He was extraordinary, giving 80,000 piasters yearly to the needy. Yet, the cruel-hearted governor remained unmoved and ordered the hanging of Salcedo at midnight. Officials sent experts to gather the confiscated silver after the execution. However, when they cast the metal into the fire, it turned to ash—leading some to believe it was a sign of divine intervention.

The Bono mine, which was once a source of Salcedo's wealth, became inundated with water and was ultimately sunk and destroyed. This was not the end of the supernatural occurrences. Fifteen days after Salcedo's unjust hanging, the governor saw in his bedroom the man he had condemned. This caused him to tremble in fear. His wife asked what the matter was. He told her what he had seen. This haunting vision ultimately led to the governor's own demise, as he fell ill and passed away within six days.

The judge who had ordered Salcedo's execution also faced divine retribution, as his hands and legs became paralyzed. These were but a few of the miraculous events that unfolded in the wake of Salcedo's tragic fate.

Salcedo's legacy, however, transcended the physical realm. He had been a true philanthropist, caring for orphans and widows, tending to the poor and destitute, and bestowing gifts upon monasteries. In his last days, a poor man from Spain sought Salcedo's help. He wanted to discuss how he could support his large, impoverished family. When Salcedo learned the poor man had been his companion on the journey, he was moved. He summoned his treasurer over and said, "Take this poor man to the treasury and let him take as many silver coins [paras] as he wants."

Reaching the treasury, the poor man took only twelve paras. Each para was worth 1,300 piasters. He left, invoking blessings upon his benefactor.

Salcedo asked his treasurer, "How many silver paras did this poor man take?"

The treasurer replied, "Twelve."

He then asked the poor man why he did not take more, but the man simply thanked him and left.

Salcedo had many examples of kind acts.

The news of Salcedo's unjust execution caused deep trouble for the king and the Inquisition. They lost a man who was guided by a "lucky star" in his unwavering compassion and contributions to the royal treasury. The king responded by issuing an order to provide Salcedo's missing brother, Don Gaspar de Salcedo, with 50,000 piasters from the royal treasury and granting him permission to reopen the Bono mine.

Elias, though unable to witness Salcedo's last moments, had the privilege of befriending his brother, Don Gaspar. Don Gaspar and his team of one hundred men worked tirelessly to drain the water from the Bono mine. He invited Elias to stay and promised to provide him with as much silver as God decreed. But Elias' pressing need to return to Spain, where his deposed friend the viceroy was also returning, prevented him from accepting Don Gaspar's offer.

Chapter 19

Legend of King Inca

Elias and his companions traveled to Chucuito after leaving the mine. There, the governor, Don Andreas de Bernajia, the nephew of the king's secretary, greeted them. The town had a royal house for coining silver, along with experts who oversaw the silver production from nearby mines. They melted the silver, minted coins stamped with the king's insignia, and confiscated any raw silver not processed by the mint for the king's treasury.

Toward one end of this town was Lake Titicaca, the legendary area of the ancient Inca civilization. Elias walked along the shores of the shimmering lake, its vast expanse stretching about sixty parsangs in circumference and sparkling like a jewel in the fading light. As the sun dipped low over the horizon, he suddenly noticed Victor appeared from a distance.

"Hello, Padre," Victor said when he reached Elias, a glint of mischief in his eye. "It's good to see you again." Elias in return greeted Victor, who wasted no time giving him a tour of the area. "You see that lake? Legend has it that the Indians once tossed a golden chain belonging to King Inca into its depths after the Spaniards killed him. Supposedly, four thousand men carried that chain, creating a ring around the town for sport. Those who fell outside the chain faced laughter and mockery from the Indians. Unfortunately, we have lost the exact location of the chain in the lake.

He pointed across the lake. "See that island? It was inhabited by pagan Indians who worshipped a mountain known as the Red Mountain. They did not use money, only a barter system. No one dared approach them; they were fierce warriors, armed with spears and arrows, known for staging raids on the Spaniards."

Elias listened intently, envisioning the clashes between cultures. "Were they not afraid?" he asked, curiosity piqued.

"Fearless, it seems," Victor replied. "They captured Spaniards, even stole male mules for food. But the governor had a plan. He called upon the village heads to gather a force—some four thousand strong. They constructed forty rafts, filled them with dirt and horses, and set out across the lake."

As they walked, the story unfolded.

"When they neared the island, the Indians were ready, arrows raining down like a storm. But the Spaniards were not without their weapons. They responded with gunfire, casting sacks of dirt onto the muddy shores to create a path for their horses."

Elias was captivated, his mind racing with images of the battle. "What happened next?"

"Upon reaching the land, the horsemen charged, cutting through the ranks of the Indians. They captured around three hundred, not counting women and children. The battle was fierce—six hundred fell that day."

The weight of history hung in the air as Elias absorbed the gravity of the events. "And what became of the captives?" he inquired.

"The governor sought the bishop of Cuzco to instruct them in the ways of Christ, to baptize them, and then to disperse them throughout the land."

The ripples of the lake whispered stories of the past as they continued their walk along the shore. These stories were a reminder of the complex tapestry of human interaction, woven through barter, conquest, and faith.

Elias stayed in that town for eight days, then set out on a journey to a village two days away, known as Cumata. Within its borders stood a monastery belonging to the Augustinians, home to the revered icon of Our Lady, the Virgin Mary, called Copacabana. This miraculous icon attracted visitors from afar, each seeking blessings from the Immaculate Queen. Eager to receive her grace, Elias made his way to the monastery, filled with hope and reverence.

After his visit, he continued to Barancilavacan, unaware that four thieves were lurking behind him, intent on robbing him of his mounts and mules. Just as their plans unfolded, an unknown force blinded the would-be robbers, thwarting their intentions. Virgin Mary intervened, blinding the would-be robbers and thwarting their intentions. Elias felt a surge of gratitude, crediting the Virgin Mary's powers for this protection.

When Elias arrived in Barancilavacan, Don Elia, the local ruler and a friend, warmly greeted him. Accompanied by priests and townsfolk, they welcomed him into his home. The following day, the bishop of the Indians visited Elias with troubling news: the governor imprisoned seven Indians for minor infractions. Elias, moved by compassion and a sense of justice, took it upon himself to address the situation. Armed with a paper bearing the names of the imprisoned men, he made his way to the prison. He approached the jailer, who complied with his request to open the gate. One by one, the prisoners were called out and freed.

When the governor learned of Elias's actions, he expressed his gratitude, saying, "May it be an offering on your behalf, for you have honored us with your visit."

Elias felt a deep sense of fulfillment. He recognized the importance of acts of kindness and justice in a world where the vulnerable were often overlooked. As for the governor, he had an ambition to craft a small domed bath from a marble stone nearby, which glimmered like crystal. He intended the stone as a gift for the king of Spain, but he passed away before realizing his dream.

Chapter 20

Illegally Gathered Wealth

Eight days after his encounter at Lake Titicaca, Elias set out for the town of Sicasica, which was administered by the men of his friend, the local governor. Elias had previously loaned the governor two thousand piastres back in Lima.

As Elias approached Sicasica, he noticed a large lake about half a parsang long on the side of the road. The governor joined Elias, and they spent the evening hunting birds in the tranquil waters until dusk fell. As he entered the town, Elias received a warm welcome and then alighted at the governor's residence. The local priests and commoners all came to greet him, for Sicasica was home to both Spanish settlers and indigenous Andeans.

The townsfolk soon informed Elias about a remarkable incident that had occurred four years earlier. A priest devotedly lived and prayed in the town's temple for over twenty years. However, people discovered the priest had improperly amassed a great deal of wealth during his time there. On his deathbed, the priest confessed and made a will, revealing the location of two buried earthenware jars. One jar contained silver, while the other held gold. He designated his brother, a priest named Don Josef (the Arabic "Yûsuf"), and his sister Doña Inez as the beneficiaries.

After the priest's passing, his relatives removed the body

from the house, locked the door, and sealed it. A delegation of authorities then arrived to exhume the hidden treasure. But to everyone's astonishment, the jars contained only blood, not a single dinar.

The local bishop had decreed that they should keep quiet about this miraculous turn of events, which showed divine justice against the priest's ill-gotten gains. The strange incident captivated and worried the people of Sicasica. Elias listened intently, fascinated by this tale of the priest's hidden hoard and the supernatural twist that had unfolded. It was a vivid illustration of the moral complexities and power dynamics at play in the colonial Andes.

Eight days later, Elias embarked on his journey to Oruro, a town he hoped to reach in five days. The road was treacherous, and he endured great hardships along the way. Upon arriving, the Jesuits welcomed him and offered him shelter. Don Alonso del Coral, the governor with an unpleasant demeanor and peculiar tastes, was known for his diet of beef tripe.

"The governor here is Don Alonso del Coral," one of the Jesuits said, a hint of disdain in his voice. "He's not a pleasant man—only eats beef tripe."

Elias chuckled softly, intrigued by the colorful description of the governor. He learned that just three parsangs away lay a silver mine, renowned for its wealth. "They extract silver without mercury here," the Jesuit continued. "It's illegal in other mines, but this place is exceptional."

With a sense of purpose, Elias visited the mine and purchased raw silver for five hundred piasters, eager to see the wonders it held. After eight days, he resumed his journey toward Potosi, feeling the weight of his mission. As night fell on the first leg of his journey, Elias sought refuge in an Indian village. He carried an order that authorized mules to be assigned to him from village to village, a privilege he wielded like royalty.

Approaching the village chief, he handed over the money and requested the mules be ready by one o'clock after midnight.

Yet, as dawn broke and sunlight spilled across the landscape, the mules were nowhere to be found. Frustration gnawed at him, and he dispatched a search party. They returned with the chief, stumbling and clearly intoxicated.

"Why were the mules not ready?" Elias asked, addressing him in Spanish.

The chief responded in his native tongue, his words slurred and unintelligible. After several failed attempts, and in a moment of anger, Elias ordered the Indians tie him to a pillar and flog him. At the first blow, the chief gasped and pleaded, suddenly spoke Spanish and said, "The mules are tethered at my place!"

Elias paused, struck by the chief's revelation. "Why did you not speak earlier?" he demanded. "Why did you wait until after the first strike?"

The chief's eyes reflected a bitter truth. "We Indians do not respond to Spaniards until they beat us."

This answer shook Elias, and he continued on his journey, his thoughts heavy with the weight of injustice. He soon arrived at Tarapaya, a place where hot water bubbled from the earth, infused with the pungent smell of phosphorus. Sick people traveled from far and wide to soak in its healing waters.

Six days later, Elias finally reached Potosi. The governor came out to meet him, accompanied by ten men from his retinue, extending a warm welcome from a mile away. Elias learned that this governor, who was related to the governor general's wife, had been instructed to treat him well.

Settling into the Jesuit residence, Elias found himself surrounded by visitors eager to hear his stories. He also ventured out to visit others.

Chapter 21

Silver-Bearing Stones

One day, Elias visited the place where the Spanish colonial authorities minted their coinage—dinars, piastres, half-piastres, and quarter-piastres. This mint housed forty black slaves and twelve Spaniards who worked tirelessly to produce these coins. Elias noticed coin piles, sorted by value, scattered on the floor and trampled. Piastres in one area, half-piastres in another, and quarter-piastres in yet another, like worthless dirt.

The famous mountain, containing the silver mine, lay on the outskirts of town. This mountain was renowned throughout the world for its extraordinary wealth, with countless treasures extracted from its four sides over the past 140 years. The mine underwent deep excavation by the Spanish, who extracted maximum silver from its depths. They built supports to prevent the mountain from collapsing inward, while they mostly hollowed out the inside.

Around 700 indigenous Andean workers toiled in the mine, extracting silver-rich stone for Spanish miners who obtained rights from the Crown. The mines required villages to send men. They selected one out of every five men. The colonial governor-general could depose local rulers who objected.

Once the indigenous workers arrived in Potosí, the governor would assign them to different mine operations. This reinforced the exploitative silver extraction system that played a vital role in the Spanish colonial economy in the Andes.

Elias spotted Victor leaning against a massive mill, a knowing smile on his face.

"Welcome to the heart of Potosi," Victor said, gesturing to the bustling operation. "This is where silver is forged from the earth."

Elias observed the intricate workings of the mills. "What's the process here?"

Victor straightened up, his enthusiasm palpable. "The silver-bearing stones are ground finely in thirty-seven mills that operate day and night, except on Sundays and holidays. After grinding, the material is piled up, and then water and mercury are added to initiate the extraction process."

"Interesting. How do they know when the mixture is just right?" Elias inquired.

"They scoop samples, wash them, and smear them on clay pots. If it crumbles, it's too hot; if it sticks, it's too cold. When it adheres and shines, that's the ideal state."

Elias reflected on a story from his past. "I had a friend whose father once had the Indians dismantle a non-silver mine. After thirty-seven years, he reopened it and found that the stones had transformed, bearing silver."

"Ah, the influence of the planet Mercury, as they say. It's a fascinating idea," Victor replied, nodding. "There's a lot of folklore surrounding these mountains."

As they walked away from the mills, Elias learned more about the town's wealth.

"There are four prominent men here who operate the mint, producing vast quantities of piasters and paying substantial taxes to the king," Victor said, then pointed to a nearby lake. "And just down the road is a lake that once flooded the town, destroying many homes. Yet the people persevered, as they always do."

Elias absorbed the weight of these stories, understanding the resilience of the inhabitants. "Such harsh realities."

"Precisely," Victor agreed. "And that's why understanding their stories is so important."

With a nod, Elias decided it was time to continue his journey. "I'm heading to Chuquis soon. I'll meet you later."

"Safe travels, Padre," Victor replied.

Elias ended up remaining in this town for forty-five days before he set off toward his next destination. The sun cast long shadows behind him, illuminating the path ahead. On the first day of his journey, he reached a place where hot springs sprang forth from the earth—known to the Spanish as Los Baños Calientes. He spent the night there before proceeding to Chuquisaca the next day.

Upon his arrival in Chuquisaca, the Jesuits, who took him to their residence warmly welcomed Elias. This town served as the seat of the Spanish colonial government, with a governor and royal overseers reporting to the Viceroy of Lima. It was also home to a bishop who received an annual allocation of 126,000 piasters—an impressive sum.

Shortly after settling in, the bishop visited Elias, and the two quickly developed a friendly rapport. The chief Inquisitor, a priest named Don Bartolomé de Bavida, also befriended Elias through the governor, who was a close friend of his. The bishop even sent two priests to call on him, further enhancing his connections in the town.

Eight days into his stay, Elias reciprocated the visits from the priests, friars, and commoners who saw him. Twelve days later, the bishop invited him to celebrate mass in the cathedral on Apostles' Day. Equipped with the vestments and implements from Pope Clement IX, Elias gladly accepted. The council's leader later invited him to conduct mass in their church, a distinction he appreciated.

As time went on, heads of local monasteries and convents approached Elias, requesting him to hold mass in their institutions. One Jesuit even asked him to visit his ailing sister, for whom Elias prescribed a treatment of frog ashes that ultimately cured her. He also received special dispensation to enter a convent to treat a sick nun, who likewise recovered under his care. Elias attributed all their healing to God's grace.

Elias impressed the townspeople of Chuquisaca and urged him to stay, even offering to pay him five hundred piasters per year to cover his expenses. However, Elias politely declined, making it clear that he did not intend to remain permanently. His journey through colonial Spanish America would continue onward.

Chapter 22

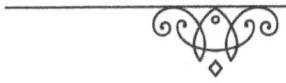

Tucuman and Buenos Aires

Elias al-Mu'sili journeyed through the regions of Tucuman and Buenos Aires. The bishop of Tucuman was a friend and companion from Spain. He urged Elias to venture to the distant lands of Tucuman, located some five hundred parasangs from the town of Chuquis. He promised Elias a thousand mules if he would make the journey, as animals were plentiful and of little value in those rugged mountains. Elias declined the offer, wary of the vast distances.

The region was home to many Indian tribes living in the vast mountain ranges. Elias feared the indigenous groups, causing them to avoid traveling through the area rich in valuable natural resources like gold, silver, and precious gemstones. However, the overall population inhabiting this region was relatively sparse.

Within this vast territory lay a district called Santa Fe, known for its emerald mining operations. The bishopric, or ecclesiastical jurisdiction, of this area encompassed an impressive 1,500 miles of land. On one end of this region sat the port town of Buenos Aires, on the ocean near the borders of Brazil, which was under the rule of the Portuguese. The locals in this town cultivated and harvested an herb called "Yerba de Pales". It was widely consumed by the population, who prepared it by boiling it with sugar and hot water.

Elias was happy to see Victor in this town. Through the guide's witty and insightful guidance, he wanted to know more about this herb.

"One cup is enough to benefit a person," Victor said. "But if the drinker wants to regurgitate, drinking more than one cup will force everything out of his stomach. This is common among all the people of that land, like coffee in your country."

Elias listened, nodding his head.

"Now, let's head south to a town called Misque. It's home to Indians, Spaniards, a governor, and a priest," Victor explained. "In Misque, there's also a bishop, a king's council of state, and they're in constant conflict with the Indians and pagans, before they acquired warfare skills."

"What do you mean?" Elias asked.

"The Indians learned about modern war tactics after associating with Spaniards. Before that, they had no horses, nor did they know how to ride them. Now they ride horses bearing spears, like Arabs, and constantly combat with Spaniards. Should they capture one, they would barbecue and eat his flesh. As for the head, they hollow out the skull and make a drinking vessel out of it, and drink one of the wines of their country with it. They are defiant, fierce, and cruel."

This frightened Elias.

"I understand your trepidation, but you see, this place has a Jesuit stronghold," Victor remarked, gesturing to the sprawling terrain. "They've practically claimed it as their own. They believed they were elevating these tribes, teaching them agriculture and culture. A noble mission was their perspective." He adopted a more serious tone. "They believed they were saving souls, civilizing the so-called 'barbaric peoples.' Scholars like Moratori and Bovon praised their efforts. But the indigenous response was mixed."

Elias nodded, understanding the complexity. "Many resist their influence, didn't they?"

"Exactly," Victor replied. "While the Jesuits sought to uplift and educate, the indigenous populations fought to maintain their cultural autonomy. There were uprisings and conflicts—real struggles against foreign domination."

Elias listened intently as they passed through the lush landscapes. "It seems the relationship was fraught with tension."

"Very much so," Victor acknowledged. "The Indians' fathers and grandfathers opposed the opposition. Some fled this country after their kings were killed, and they lived in the high and rugged mountains. And yet, the Jesuits did manage to create self-sustaining communities in some areas. It's a complicated legacy."

As they approached the town of Misque, Victor pointed out the mix of Spanish and indigenous inhabitants. "Here, the Spanish settlers were often at war with local tribes, who learned quickly how to fight back. It's a brutal history."

"Indeed, a grim reality," Victor said, his voice low. "But amidst all this, you once gifted a cherished icon of Christ's face to a local Jesuit. What happened to it?"

Elias sighed, recalling the puzzling events after returning to Potosi. "I found the icon in my belongings again, as if it had returned to me. But when the head of the Mercedarian monastery requested it, I agreed—and it never came back."

"Guess it might be living it up in a monastery somewhere," said Victor, smirking.

Chapter 23

The Deposed Viceroy

Elias's journey took a dramatic turn as he found himself immersed in the political turmoil surrounding the viceroy of Lima. The viceroy had been deposed without any fault of his own, and the king ordered the bishop of Lima to take his place. Ironically, this bishop, whom Elias had helped promote to the bishopric, became a formidable enemy after the viceroy's removal.

The viceroy's downfall stemmed from vicious petitions written by merchants in the Indies, aimed at both the king and his brother, Don Juan of Austria. Don Juan, a known adversary of the viceroy and a supporter of the queen, played a pivotal role in his deposition.

Elias had left Potosi accompanied by a man seeking an accounting from the deposed viceroy. Their journey led them to a town called Iquique, nestled near the Pacific Ocean. As they approached the town around midnight, their mules strayed, making for a restless night. Elias, anxious since he was carrying a load of pure silver, breathed a sigh of relief the next morning when they found the animals unharmed.

Upon entering Iquique, Elias encountered the bishop, who had recently returned from Panama. The bishop welcomed him warmly, treating him like a brother and showing him genuine kindness. During their conversation, Elias learned of an Indian who owned a rich mine that remained hidden from the Spaniards. This man and his son secretly extracted silver-laden stones at night, purifying them at home. When Elias heard that the Indian had offered forty thousand piasters for a mass, he invited him to his place.

"Tell me," Elias said, "why didn't you reveal this mine to the king? He could have been kind to you and your children, offering gifts and positions in this town."

The Indian replied, "I saw Indians older than myself who revealed such secrets to the Spaniards, only to die under their tortures. That is the reason."

Elias believed him. He had witnessed the cruelty the Spaniards inflicted upon the native people.

After ten days in Iquique, the group finally located a ship and set sail for Lima. The journey took eight days, and as they approached the port of El Callao, Elias felt a mix of relief and apprehension. He carried raw silver that, in anyone else's baggage, would have been confiscated for the king. Fortunately, no one questioned his load.

Arriving in Lima in the carriage of his friend, the head of the Inquisition, Elias learned of the bishop's actions against the judge who had come to account for the viceroy. The bishop had imprisoned the judge, declaring, "First you exile the deposed governor general, then you listen to the complaints of the inhabitants."

The governor general was brought forth to hear his order of exile. He accepted it, aware that Spanish law required a deposed governor to be exiled only six miles away. However, due to Don Juan's influence, he was exiled six hundred miles to a desolate place called Payta, where water had to be transported from miles away. His wife and servants remained outside Lima, too ill to join him.

Elias accompanied the governor to Callao, along with a few friends, to bid him farewell. The viceroy, a man of deep faith, said, "If they give me poison to drink, it would not harm me because of the strength of the Lord and His holy and pure mother."

After the carriage departed, Elias visited the bishop, questioning how God could allow such a harsh exile. "He is weak, and doctors say anyone sent to such a hot place will die! Our Lord Jesus Christ commands us to act mercifully. We care for the sick; we do not cast them out to face death!"

The bishop replied coldly, "I am angry with his wife for cursing me, so I wanted my vengeance by exiling her husband."

Before parting, the governor had asked Elias to watch over his home and wife, fearing that his enemies might poison her. For over a year, Elias fulfilled this promise, ensuring her safety while the bishop delayed the judge's accounting for seven months.

During the viceroy's exile, Elias received an unexpected summons from the bishop. As he entered the bishop's chambers, he was met with a proposition. "Why are you so closely identified with this man?" the bishop asked. "Come over to my side and leave him. I will allow you to live with me and support your interests, assisting you in all that you need."

Elias stood firm and replied, "How can I abandon an old friend and forsake his virtuous friendship? God has commanded us to help the weak and lift the fallen." One who is born in uprightness, knows his origins, and respects honor does not abandon a friend in isolation; rather, he helps and consoles him in his affliction. Yet I still hold you in high regard and consider you a friend as well."

"Do as you please!" the bishop retorted.

Two months later, the bishop sent for Elias again. Upon entering the town, Elias sought out his friend, the head Inquisitor, to share the news. The Inquisitor urged him to speak his mind to the bishop.

When Elias visited the bishop, he was met with a blunt suggestion. "Why don't you go back to your country?" the bishop asked.

Elias responded, "If I wished to do so, nothing would prevent me. At the moment, I have no intention of leaving."

The bishop pressed on, "The order you received and the permission granted are valid for four years, which are now complete."

"True," Elias conceded, "but I do not wish to leave and be parted from the viceroy. You can do as you please."

"Why do you defend this man but not accord me the same loyalty?" the bishop challenged.

Elias replied earnestly, "In our country, we protect those who are down and assist them, in keeping with God's commandment: 'Love thy neighbor as thyself.' I hold affection for both you and the viceroy, as if you were my kin."

Moved, the bishop rose from his chair, embraced Elias, and said, "God bless you; you are of noble lineage; your blood and deeds testify to that."

Elias returned to the head Inquisitor and told of the encounter. The Inquisitor rejoiced, sharing in the moment of triumph. The viceroy's wife, upon hearing the news, thanked the person and prayed for blessings upon them, their parents, and their lineage.

Finally, during Holy Week, the judge hastened to pass judgment, declaring the deposed governor general legally innocent. When the bishop learned of this, he was filled with sorrow, tearing his clothes in anguish.

The governor general returned to Lima, greeted with joy and celebration by nobles and commoners alike. His safe return was marked by great rejoicing, and the Lord blessed him with a son, whom he named Ferdinand della Cura Contde de Castilla y Marquese de Malagon.

Chapter 24

Return to Panama

Shortly thereafter, Elias left the town and traveled to a village called Madalena, located a mile away. There, his friend, the head of the Inquisition, had a lovely home and garden. Elias spent five months waiting for Spanish ships, using the time to write a record of his travels.

When the ships finally arrived, a new viceroy came with them. Elias felt a wave of disappointment; he had spent six years in the country due to his exiled friend, who had promised to expedite Elias's affairs once he regained power. With the arrival of the new viceroy, those hopes seemed dashed.

When the Spanish ships arrived in Portobelo, the bishop of Lima, who was in charge of the Peruvian territory at the time, instructed the merchants of Lima to move the king's treasury onto the royal ships. They were to journey to Portobelo and bring back seasonal goods. According to the laws, when the galleons arrived in Portobelo from Spain, they were to continue to Panama. Silver would then be transported from Panama to Portobelo by around a thousand mules, a process taking about a month over eighteen parsangs. Halfway, they would cross the small river Chagres using boats called "chatas."

Elias departed with the deposed viceroy, accompanied by notables and nobility who came to bid him farewell. Merchants joined them, all heading to the seasonal market. The day was marked by celebration, cannon fire, and fireworks, occurring on September 21, 1681. They set sail from Callao, heading toward Panama.

Five days later, they reached a port called Amotapé, where they bought provisions—chickens for one and a half piasters and ewes for five. After two days, they departed again, and three days at sea brought them to Amortajada, known for its shallow waters that often pushed ships off course. Just as they faced danger, Elias and his companions prayed fervently. The priest absolved them as they implored the Lord and the Virgin Mary for help.

Miraculously, a wind arose from the heart of the mountain, pushing their ship back to safe waters. Ships behind them, surprised by the calm seas, watched as they were driven forward by the newfound wind. This wind guided them until late afternoon the next day. Then, they entered the port of Santa Elena where they waited eleven days for a ship from Guayaquil. The ship was known as the gold ship and it was carrying twelve million in gold.

When the general arrived, he ordered them to leave the port, and they set off for Panama. They entered the port safely after having departed from Lima forty-two days earlier. There, they encountered two ships carrying Spanish soldiers sent to track down sea bandits—pirates of the South Sea.

Elias's friend, the deposed viceroy, suggested that Elias go to the New World. His inability to fulfill his promise left him feeling ashamed. To make up for it, he offered to provide Elias with everything he needed, including letters of recommendation to the viceroy of the New World, who happened to be a relative of his.

With renewed purpose, Elias prepared to record the news of his journey to the New World, trusting in the help of God Almighty for success.

Chapter 25

Soloman's Island

In December of 1681, Elias and his companions embarked on a large vessel called the "Captain," traveling nine miles to the island of Taboga. They spent three days there gathering provisions—vegetables, fruits, and refreshments—before setting off for the port of Realejo.

Five days into their journey, they encountered an uninhabited island known as Montuosa. There, the winds died down, and the ship remained still for twelve days. Nearby lay Isla de los Ladrones, or "the island of thieves." Elias recalled stories of a ship that had been driven by crosswinds to this sandy isle while attempting to reach the New World. The sailors, needing to repair their galley, collected sand to fill their cooking basin. The next day, when the cook prepared the meals, he discovered that the sand had turned to stone, revealing a nugget of gold.

Elias learned that the sailors had hoped to return to the island but were unable to do so, lacking precise information about its location. Legend had it that this island was referred to as Isla de Solomon, a place from which King Solomon supposedly sourced gold for his temple.

"Why are the Spaniards disinterested in searching for it?" Elias asked the general.

The general clarified that there is no confirmed Solomon's Island in Panama. He further explained that references to such an island usually pertain to legends and historical accounts rather than a specific, verified location. The stories surrounding these islands are largely considered mythological rather than factual."

Shortly thereafter, the winds shifted, allowing them to leave. Three days later, they arrived at Golfo Dulce, or "the sweet gulf," where a freshwater river mingled with the sea. They dropped anchor, and the sailors went ashore to replenish their water supply. Elias joined them, eager to cool off in the cold waters of the river, which was only about a yard deep. He noticed flecks of gold mixed with the sand and showed it to the ship's captain, who was familiar with the region.

"Don't be surprised," the captain said. "There is gold to be found in all these lands and rivers, but the Spaniards do not dare extract it because of the pagan Indians inhabiting the mountains."

While anchored, a sudden turbulence caused the sea to swell, breaking the anchor rope twice. After three days, they set sail again, reaching a port called La Caldera, or "the pot," six days later. Elias asked the soldiers on the ship to gather some shells. They returned with nine, and as he opened them, he discovered a pearl the size of a chickpea in one.

"How contemptible!" he exclaimed. "There are pearls in this sea, and you do not attempt to dive for them."

The general replied, "This too is because of our fear of pagan Indians."

They spent one day in port, enduring hot rain and still winds. Five days later, they approached a mountain called Papagayo. As they neared it, a powerful wind blew, shattering the mast into three pieces. Despair filled their hearts as they faced the raging sea, fearing for their salvation. But through the power of the Almighty Deliverer, the sea calmed, and the wind gradually died down, restoring hope to Elias and his companions.

Six days later, they reached the port of Realejo and disembarked. They spent a full day and night there. The general took the opportunity to write a letter to the bishop of the city of Leon, which is located about twenty-seven miles away. In the letter, he informed the bishop about Elias's arrival. The bishop was overjoyed upon hearing the news, having become friends with Elias in Paris. The bishop, a monk from the order of Mercy, resolved a dispute with the Parisian monks and was then appointed to the bishopric in Madrid by the king.

The next day, Elias set off for the city of Leon. His happiness grew as he noticed the bishop emerging to greet him from a distance of six miles. The bishop welcomed him into his home, where he spent eight days as a guest. During his stay, Elias reconnected with a friend he had met in Lima, who gifted him a fine female mule. The bishop also presented Elias with a gift of his own.

They left after eight days and traveled to a town called Salvajo, which was two parsangs away. From there, they continued to another town known as Nostra Señora del Viejo, meaning "Our Lady of the Old" in Spanish. This Virgin was renowned for her miracles, especially among travelers at sea.

In the midst of a turbulent sea, Elias made a vow. He promised to hold mass for nine days in Her honor if he reached Her church. He remained in Nostra Señora del Viejo for nineteen days, fulfilling his vow. During this time, he awaited a sunbûk, a skiff called a canoa, to cross the narrow sea, which spanned about thirty-four parsangs.

The bishop had warned Elias against crossing this dangerous stretch of water, as many ships had sunk there. However, Elias placed his faith in the Virgin Mary, whom he affectionately referred to as "the daughter of my country," and decided to embark on the sunbûk despite the risks.

Chapter 26

San Salvator, Guatemala

After a grueling twenty-hours through the narrows, Elias and his companions successfully reached the other side. They disembarked in a small village called Amapala, which consisted of only four houses inhabited by Indians. There, Elias encountered a Spaniard traveling from the New World to Peru. Determined to cross the narrows, the man sold his horse to an Indian for two and a half piasters. The deal included the horse's saddle and bridle.

They left Amapala and traveled for eight days, eventually arriving at an Indian village called Amushayu. From there, they continued on to San Miguel and then to Zuruaquin. Their journey took them through various villages until they arrived at Cuquinbit and then to San Martin.

As Elias wandered through the bustling market of San Martin, admiring the vibrant textiles dyed with indigo, he was startled by the sudden appearance of a tall figure. It was Victor, the tour guide, effortlessly weaving through the crowd, his voice carrying over the sounds of haggling and laughter.

"Welcome to San Martin!" he exclaimed, gesturing grandly. "Let me show you the stories hidden within these streets."

Elias's eyes lit up at the sight of Victor. With a broad smile, he said, "What a nice surprise! I always enjoy a good tour. Please, lead the way."

"In the 1600s," Victor started, his engaging and informative tone accompanied by his Latin accent. He described San Martin as a small agricultural settlement surrounded by lush landscapes and rolling hills. Picture fertile valleys, where the indigenous communities thrived, cultivating crops like maize and beans. And then there's the indigo plant, known locally as 'nili.' This plant, resembling trefoil, was essential for dye production."

He paused, allowing Elias to take in the scene. "Remarkably, nili could grow as tall as a person. The locals harvested it and fermented the leaves in large basins, stirring the mixture until it foamed. They formed the foam into balls, drying them in the sun. Quite the process, isn't it? They called it 'testicular nile'—a name that certainly grabs one's attention!"

Elias chuckled, intrigued. "And the plant was primarily for dye, not food?"

"Exactly," Victor replied with a nod. "While the indigo leaves contain indican, which creates that beautiful blue dye, they aren't typically eaten. Livestock like cattle and horses can nibble on it, but in moderation—too much can be toxic. So, it's not a primary food choice for them."

Continuing through the village, Victor pointed to the simple thatched-roof homes made from local materials. "These mud-walled houses blend seamlessly into the landscape. Livestock grazes in the fields, while farmers work alongside family and neighbors. San Martin served as a crossroads for traders and travelers, bustling with a market where local goods, including those vibrant textiles, were exchanged."

He gestured to the sound of church bells echoing in the distance. "Churches, often modest, stood as central gathering places, reflecting the strong Catholic influence of the Spanish colonial period. Those bells marked the rhythm of village life, reminding everyone of the time and the sacred."

Elias turned to Victor. "I've heard about the Mayan ruins in this region. What can you tell me about them?"

Victor smiled, eager to share. "Ah, the Mayan ruins! They are a fascinating testament to an advanced civilization. The Mayans built remarkable cities like Tikal and Quiriguá, flourishing from around 250 AD to 900 AD. These sites are filled with impressive pyramids and intricate carvings that tell the stories of their gods, rulers, and daily life."

"What was the significance of these temples?" Elias asked.

"Great question! The temples served multiple purposes—religious ceremonies, astronomical observations, and even as tombs for their rulers. They were central to Mayan culture, acting as a hub for both spiritual and civic life."

As they continued walking, Elias's brow furrowed in thought. "You know, these temples resemble the ziggurats in Mesopotamia. They both serve similar purposes—worship, rituals, and connecting with the divine."

"Yes, that is true," said Victor, a twinkle in his eyes. The ziggurats were constructed between 2200 BCE and 500 BCE, serving as monumental structures for religious and civic purposes in ancient Iraq. On the other hand, the Mayan temples were built from 250 CE to 900 CE and functioned as sites for ceremonies and royal tombs. He grinned. "Maybe there were aliens involved. You know, intergalactic architects sharing design tips across the ages."

Elias laughed, shaking his head. "Aliens aside, it's remarkable how different cultures can arrive at similar architectural solutions. It makes you wonder about the shared human experience."

"Exactly!" Victor replied. "Despite the distance and differences, humanity has always sought to reach for the divine in similar ways. It's one of the great unifying themes of our history."

They walked in silence, Elias pondering the architectural similarities between ancient ziggurats of Mesopotamia and Mayan temples of Mesoamerica, despite their cultural differences.

After this enlightening tour, Elias felt inspired. He bid farewell to Victor and moved on to a village called Jalaya, followed by Santa Ana. His journey continued to the village of Tekesa, known for its Mulato population, the offspring of white fathers and black mothers, each with their unique blend of complexions. The exploration of this rich cultural tapestry excited Elias as he ventured through Kiliyataco, Escalaos, and Paytapa, eventually reaching Santiago, known as Saint Jacob.

In Santiago, he arrived in Guatemala, the seat of the king's government, known as Audiencia, presided over by a man called presidente. Here, he met the wealthy bishop, Don Juan de Ortega. After a warm visit, Elias conducted mass in the church, even in the presence of the bishop's confessor, without prior permission. The bishop, pleased with Elias's vestments—a gift from the pope—requested that two priests attend his masses.

Elias spent thirty-four days in Guatemala, where he was generously treated by the locals, holding mass in various churches and monasteries. During this time, he received many suitable gifts. Shortly after Lent began in 1682, Elias prepared to leave the town. The sergeant of arms of the Audiencia and four priests accompanied him for about a mile outside the city to bid farewell.

Continuing his journey, Elias traveled to Chatamalina Bejacu, followed by Basun and then Basima Tuluz. He made his way to San Antonio de Suchitepec, where he learned of local governance issues. The district was overseen by an official from Seville, against whom the Indians had lodged complaints. Elias interceded on the official's behalf, writing to Don Juan Miguel de Agurto, a supportive and staunch Christian leader.

From this region, Elias noted, cacao was cultivated and transformed into chocolate. The cocoa trees were abundant, tended by wealthy Indians who had set aside substantial funds to cover legal disputes with local authorities.

Elias continued onward, visiting various villages like Tapu, Santa Maria de Belen, and San Cristobal. His travels took him through many communities, each with its own unique culture and practices, further enriching his understanding of the land he traversed.

Arriving in Chiapa, Elias became entangled in a bitter dispute between the bishop and the leader of the Dominican order. The governor was excommunicated by the bishop, causing a significant divide between religious and political powers. Elias aimed to bring together the conflicting parties, saddened by their discord. He tirelessly worked with both the bishop and the Provincial to find a resolution. Acting as a peacemaker, Elias successfully brought the bishop, the Provincial, and the governor together on the Virgin Mary's birthday. He reminded them of Jesus Christ's command to be at peace, and through his impassioned plea, he successfully brokered a reconciliation.

The governor and bishop showed their appreciation by giving gifts, while the priests and monks were captivated by Elias' journey from the "Old World. After spending sixteen days in Chiapa, Elias proceeded on his journey, passing through various villages such as Tosta, Ecoscaona, and ultimately Bianatic. The final village served as a significant boundary, symbolizing the shift from Mexican viceroyalty to Guatemalan governorship. Elias' peace mission led him through this threshold, symbolizing his role as a bridge between distinct realms of the Spanish empire.

Chapter 27

Journey to Mexico

Elias journeyed to the village of Sanatitipec, then on to Istinipec, and finally reached the town of Xilapa, where he was greeted by a man named Don Juan Vetia. Don Juan, a ruler of the town, was the nephew of the secretary of the Indian office and a strong ally of Elias. Upon hearing of Elias's arrival, he traveled two parsangs to meet him, welcoming him with honor and dignity. He insisted that Elias stay in his home.

Nearby, a mountain posed a danger, known for transient bandits who occasionally robbed travelers. To ensure Elias's safety, the local governor assigned two guards to accompany him across the mountain. With God's protection, they navigated the perilous terrain without harm and soon arrived at Texia.

From Texia, Elias continued to San Juan della Costa, then to Inxapa, and onward to San Miguel, before making his way to San Lucas and finally arriving in Oaxaca. In Oaxaca, he met a nobleman from Spain who had a brother in Lima. This nobleman joyfully received a letter Elias had brought for his brother and insisted that he stay in a home prepared for him.

In Oaxaca, the bishopric was temporarily vacant, overseen by a kind caretaker named Don Dionisio. This blessed man had once been captured in Algiers while traveling from India to

Spain but had been freed by divine grace. Elias had cultivated a friendship with Don Dionisio, who was exceedingly generous.

Oaxaca was rich in architecture, with numerous churches and monasteries, especially the elegant Dominican monastery. The large cathedral was adorned with silver and gold, a testament to the town's wealth. Elias carried eight hundred piasters. Some of the money was given to Don Francisco de Castro to buy kermes, a valuable dye obtained from insects that cling to specific trees.

One afternoon, as Elias strolled through the vibrant streets of Oaxaca, he noticed Victor standing beside a colorful market stall.

"Hey, Elias!" Victor called out with a welcoming smile. "I want to share some fascinating history about Oaxaca, particularly the Chaldean community."

Elias paused, curiosity piqued. "I've never heard of this. When did it happen?"

"Oh, it was after your time, but that's alright," Victor replied, gesturing toward a nearby café. "Shall we grab a coffee and continue our conversation?"

As they walked, Victor elaborated, "Many Chaldeans began arriving in Mexico in the early 1900s. An example is Anthony Shamouni who came in 1909. Dr. Ulises Casab Rueda wrote a book about their journey called *Ixtepec-Telkef*."

They arrived at the café, ordered their coffees, and sat down. Victor continued, listing other notable Chaldeans, including José Murat Casab, who served as governor of Oaxaca from 1998 to 2004. He mentioned pioneers like Dawood and George Shango, who arrived in 1926 and made a living selling textiles without knowing Spanish.

"By 1927, immigration from Iraq to Mexico had declined due to visa restrictions, leaving only fifty-five documented Chaldeans by 1929," he added, sipping his coffee. "Today,

Chaldean families are scattered across Mexico, making it difficult to form a strong community or archdiocese," Victor said. "Visits from Chaldean clergy have been rare, and there's been a significant shift toward Spanish among younger generations, with their knowledge of Chaldean-Aramaic fading."

"Are we talking 300 to 400 years from now?" Elias asked, trying to grasp the timeline.

Victor nodded, taking another sip of his coffee. "Yes, indeed, Padre. That's exactly what we're discussing."

Elias leaned back, his mind racing with the weight of history and future.

After a fifteen-day stay, Elias departed for Mexico City, where the viceroy resided. He traveled through several villages, including Ipita, Tatao, and Owanetepec, before reaching the bustling city of La Puebla de Los Angeles. This vibrant city was filled with palaces, monuments, and rich churches, including a beautifully ornate cathedral.

In Puebla, Elias stayed with a friend and learned that the current bishop, Emanuel de Santa Cruz, was a learned man of faith with an impressive annual income. The presence of various monastic orders in the city added to its spiritual and architectural richness, making it a remarkable destination on Elias's journey.

Two days later, Elias departed for Mexico City, where he had a friend waiting for him. Upon arriving, he was warmly welcomed by this friend, who received him with honor and kindness. However, the next day, Elias fell ill and remained bedridden for ten days. During this time, he carried a letter from the viceroy in Peru, a relative of the current viceroy, who had written to his governors to watch over Elias.

With God's help, Elias recovered and soon visited the viceroy and his wife, both of whom greeted him with love and smiles. The viceroy offered him a place to stay in the palace, but overwhelmed by his generosity, Elias politely declined the offer. Instead, he rented a house for three hundred sixty piasters a year and arranged for a carriage and mules at six hundred fifty piasters.

Elias began to visit the nobles of the city, starting with the bishop, who granted him permission to hold masses wherever he wished. Each evening, Elias spent about two hours chatting with the viceroy before returning home. Mexico City, situated in a lowland basin near a lake fed by springs, had a troubled history of heavy rains that once caused the city to sink, flooding many homes.

The magnificence of the city was evident in its architecture, with churches and fine edifices lining the streets. It boasted three monasteries for Franciscans, two for Dominicans, three for Augustinians, and many more, including hospitals and nunneries. The cathedral was particularly notable for its ornate decoration.

About half a mile outside the city stood the Church of the Virgin Mary of Guadalupe. Local legend tells the story of Juan Diego, an Indian who met a radiant woman after the Spaniards arrived. She instructed him to ask the bishop to build a house for her. Frightened, Juan Diego hurried to the bishop, but the man dismissed him due to his humble appearance and clothing.

Undeterred, Juan Diego returned to the same spot, where the lady appeared again, urging him to return to the bishop with a sign. She handed him a rose, out of season, and instructed him to take it to the bishop. When he arrived, the servants humiliated him, but he insisted on delivering a message from the lady.

Finally allowed in, Juan Diego presented the rose and recounted the lady's words. When he revealed the rose, the bishop was astonished to see an image of the Virgin Mary imprinted on Juan Diego's garment. Overcome with awe, the bishop fell to his knees and begged for forgiveness. The rose and garment were paraded in celebration, and the bishop ordered a church to be built on the site of the apparition.

Juan Diego spent the rest of his life serving the Virgin in that church, which was richly adorned with silver, gold, and precious robes. The church had silver steps and pillars. A causeway was built to connect it to the city, providing access during the summer rains that flooded the ground. In this region, the rainy season began in May and lasted until September, quite different from Elias's homeland.

Chapter 28

Attack of the Pirates

Elias spent about six months relaxing in the city, patiently awaiting the arrival of a ship from Spain, which would bring letters from merchants to their partners. The ship's arrival brought not just correspondence, but also a deceitful individual who falsely claimed to be dispatched by the king for crime investigation and treasury assessment. This impostor instilled fear in the hearts of many guilty individuals.

Upon hearing of this newcomer, the viceroy instructed the governor of the port to examine the orders this man possessed. However, the impostor refused to reveal any details. Realizing he was being deceived, the viceroy sent soldiers to apprehend him. They successfully captured the man, and he was subsequently imprisoned.

During this tumultuous time, pirate ships began arriving in the port of Vera Cruz. The heretical pirates, representing different factions, secretly landed about a mile and a half outside the city. They entered the unprotected port like thieves in the night. They went directly to the governor's house and took him prisoner. Soon after, they rounded up men and women, imprisoning them in the large church and locking the doors, stationing guards to keep watch.

For the next three days, the pirates plundered monasteries, churches, and homes. Once they released the prisoners from the church, they forced them to carry the stolen loot to their ships, anchored approximately three-quarters of a mile away. The pirates loaded everything—men, women, and slaves—onto their vessels and transported them to an island nearby, demanding a ransom of 150,000 piasters for their release. The captives managed to send word to the city of Puebla, and ten days later, the ransom was raised.

Ultimately, the Spaniards were freed, but the pirates kept the black slaves and an impressive haul of loot valued at eight million piasters. The pirates numbered around six hundred, while the captives exceeded four thousand. Among the pirates was a heretical chief who had a Spanish companion named Nesilio. After a quarrel over the division of the spoils, Nesilio killed the chief and assumed leadership of the pirates.

Elias, who had been in the town with a load of kermes he had purchased in Oaxaca for a thousand piasters, found that it was among the stolen treasures. However, just as the pirates settled on the island, ships from Spain arrived in port. The viceroy quickly informed the general about the situation, urging him to act decisively against the pirates before they could escape with their plunder.

The general rallied ship captains to strategize, concerned that he might be held accountable if his ships were harmed during combat. But when the time came for action, Nesilio glanced at the gathering Spanish fleet, raised his sails, and sailed away, laughing at their efforts. He took with him over two thousand captives and slaves, including some of African descent. This dramatic episode unfolded in the year 1683.

Chapter 29

From Mexico to Baghdad via China

A hundred years prior, during the reign of Philip IV, king of Spain, ships set sail from the New World, venturing toward the coasts of China. During one such journey, they stumbled upon an island, which they named the Philippines in honor of the king. Spaniards settled on this island and ships transported priests and friars to convert the indigenous population to Christianity.

Every year, a ship departed from the Philippines, laden with goods from China. The journey to the New World took eight months, but the return trip was significantly shorter, lasting only three months. These voyages were pivotal in establishing trade between the two regions, as merchants sought to connect the vast distances between the Americas and Asia.

Elias found out that ships departing from Callao port in mid-March would utilize the seasonal Alizés winds to arrive in Manila in less than two months. The return journey, however, proved much more challenging, often taking ten to twelve months. A Jesuit father had suggested utilizing the opposing winds, leading to a change in departure strategy. From July onward, ships would leave Manila, traveling north until they caught the western winds that would guide them to California and Mexico, where they would anchor in Acapulco.

Additionally, each year, a ship from Surat arrived at the

Philippines, carrying goods intended for two Armenian merchants from Julfa. These merchants loaned money to the Spaniards for a year, and when the ship returned from Surat, it collected the old debts and arranged new loans from the proceeds. No other ships were permitted to make this journey, as only those belonging to the Julfites were allowed to trade in that region.

Elias had intended to travel on one of these ships to the Philippines and then board another vessel bound for Surat before finally returning to his homeland. However, his plans took an unexpected turn when he clashed with the man who was about to take up the governorship of the Philippines. The governor requested a loan of ten thousand piasters from Elias. Concerned, Elias consulted with the viceroy, who warned him, "Beware, he is in debt and owes 200,000 piasters." Taking this advice to heart, Elias decided against this route and resolved to return to Spain instead.

Elias learned that about fifty years prior, a group of missionaries had traveled from the Philippines to China with the purpose of converting the local populace from paganism to Christianity. However, the devil, ever the adversary of good, inspired the king of China to eliminate the monks. He ordered the execution of all the missionaries who had settled in China and then dispatched a formidable armada to the Philippines.

When the inhabitants of the Philippines saw this great fleet approaching, fear gripped their hearts. They were few in number and unprepared for such an assault. With no options left, they sought refuge in the church, where they fervently prayed for divine intervention and carried the holy body in procession, hoping for deliverance from their impending doom.

By God's grace, their prayers were answered. The sea rose in fury, scattering and destroying the ships of the Chinese armada. In the end, only thirteen vessels survived the catastrophic encounter. When the king of China learned of the disaster that had befallen his fleet, he was profoundly saddened and passed away soon after.

His eldest son ascended to the throne, determined to avenge his father's defeat. He prepared a new army and fortified ships to wage war against the Philippines. Yet, as fate would have it, this expedition met the same disastrous fate as its predecessor, resulting in the total annihilation of the fleet. The young prince, overwhelmed by sorrow, also died shortly thereafter.

The throne then passed to his younger brother, who similarly sought to prepare an armed force. However, his mother cautioned him against pursuing war with the island, urging him instead to avoid the fate that had befallen his father and brother. She advised him to seek peace, to befriend the missionaries, and to allow them to enter China freely to preach the Gospel without opposition. Following her counsel, the new king opened the doors to the missionaries. Now, every three years, monks arrived from Spain, crossing over to China to teach and preach without hindrance.

Elias recalled a friend who had served as a captain in the Philippines for about seventeen years. When this friend visited Mexico and stayed with Elias, he recounted the miraculous events that had transpired in the islands. Elias trusted his friend's account, knowing him to be a truthful man. He also had the testimonies of Jesuits and monks, who corroborated the truth of the calamity that had struck the Chinese armada.

Elias had also heard tales of the Spaniards' discovery and conquest of an island close to the Philippines around fifty years ago. The island's inhabitants were originally idol-worshipping Indians, but the Spaniards converted them to Christianity and baptized them. They named the island after the queen, who was King Philippe IV's wife. They had called it the "Mariannes," after the mother of King Carlos II, Queen Marie Anne d'Autriche.

Elias recalled that when he had been in Mexico, two Dominican friars had arrived from the Philippines, bearing petitions to the Pope. These friars had accompanied Elias back to Spain on the same ship. It was then that they had shown him the petitions, seeking his support before the Pope regarding a disaster that had befallen them.

Apparently, there had been a dispute between the Jesuits and the bishop of the Philippines. The bishop had demanded taxes from the Jesuits, but they had refused to obey or pay him. In retaliation, the judges of the Philippines had seized the bishop at night, put him on a ship, and exiled him to a place some forty-five miles away. The bishop, who was a member of the Dominican order, had died in exile, much like St. John Chrysostom.

When the two Dominican friars had reached Rome and presented the petition detailing this incident to the Pope, His Eminence had been greatly disturbed by the foul deed. He had then sent word rebuking the King of Spain for the actions of his judges and the exile of the bishop. Upon learning of the matter, the King and his court had ordered the deposition and exile of the judges responsible. These judges had subsequently died in exile under this ban.

Rabbât critiqued Elias al-Mûsili's claims in his travelogue, highlighting several inaccuracies. He noted that al-Mûsili mistakenly identified a Japanese armada as Chinese and conflated various events, including persecutions in Japan, China, and Tonca. Rabbât suggested that al-Mûsili's reliance on hearsay led to unreliable sources.

Additionally, he pointed out that al-Mûsili seemed unaware that Jesuits and other religious orders were typically exempt from paying taxes to bishops. Rabbât conducted research and found no historical confirmation of al-Mûsili's account, speculating that he might have confused two separate incidents. The first involved the Jesuits in Mexico and Bishop Johannes Balafocas, who demanded taxes from them forty years before al-Mûsili's arrival; the Jesuits ultimately prevailed in this dispute.

The second incident involved Bishop Arnan Gerero of Manila, who had a conflict with the Jesuits but later reconciled with them. Rabbât also noted discrepancies in al-Mûsili's measurements and distances, suggesting they were estimates based on his travels or secondhand accounts.

Chapter 30

Return to Europe

Elias traveled from Mexico City to the port of Vera Cruz, a journey of approximately forty parsangs, as the ships readied to sail from Mexico back to Spain. There, he spoke with the general of the ships and requested passage to Spain. The general agreed, but demanded one thousand piasters in return, which would cover Elias' food and accommodation on the voyage.

This was not Elias' first time navigating the complex relationship between the Catholic Church and the Jesuit order in the Spanish colonies. He was well aware of the history of tensions, such as the conflict between the bishop of Puebla de Los Angeles, Johannes Balafocas, and the Jesuits several decades earlier. The bishop had tried to collect taxes from the Jesuits, who refused to pay, leading to a ruling by the Apostolic nuncio in favor of the Jesuits. Balafocas was subsequently ousted from the city, which he blamed on the Jesuit missions.

Elias was also familiar with the more recent dispute between the bishop of Manila, Arnan Gerero, and the Jesuits. Gerero had summoned the Manila clergy to a meeting, but the Jesuits excused themselves, angering the bishop. However, the conflict was short-lived, as Gerero soon regretted his actions and reconciled with the Jesuits.

Despite the high cost of passage, Elias had no choice but

to accept the general's terms. Eight days later, the ship captains held a council to determine whether they could set sail for Spain during the current season. Unable to leave for three more months, they sent a small ship ahead with letters and news from the colonies.

Elias grew concerned about his situation, as the port of Vera Cruz was known for its hot climate, foul water, and unpleasant conditions. He chose the small ship bound for Spain, with the initial destination of La Habana (Cuba), which served as the port for Peruvian galleys and New World ships.

In Vera Cruz, Elias found a friend who advised him to purchase two loads of dry onions and two cases of apples as gifts. Heeding this advice, Elias bought the produce and set sail. It took them twenty days to reach La Habana. When they arrived, the governor, who happened to be the brother of the general who had taken Elias to Peru, was pleasantly surprised and delighted by the unexpected gifts of onions and apples. He asked, "How do you know we need onions and apples on this island?"

When people plant onion on that island it grows to the size of a mouse's tail, Elias described in his travelogue. Elias stayed on the island for four and a half months, until the ships from the New World arrived, enjoying the island's pleasant climate and sweet water.

One day, as the sun hung high in the sky, casting a warm glow over the vibrant city, Elias walked in the street. He scanned the crowd and soon spotted a tall figure with a welcoming smile, waving enthusiastically.

"Welcome to Havana, my friend!" Victor said in his smooth and confident voice smooth and confident. Clad in a simple yet elegant outfit, he exuded an air of intelligence and charm.

"Thank you! I was hoping to see you as I'm returning home," said Elias.

"Yes, I've heard," Victor said, sadly. "Come, let's start our journey at the Castillo del Morro. It's not just a fortress; it's the guardian of our bay and a testament to our battles against pirates and invaders."

As they walked, Victor pointed out the fortress rising majestically against the azure sky. "Built to protect the city, it has seen more action than a bullfighter in a ring! Just imagine the cannon fire echoing across the bay." He walked on, gesturing to the bustling market. "Havana is a melting pot. Here, you'll find Spanish settlers, indigenous peoples, and the vibrant influence of African traditions. It's a lively dance of music, food, and faith."

They entered the market, where the air was filled with the rich scents of spices and fresh produce. Victor leaned in, a conspiratorial smile on his lips. "You see, my friend, the true treasure of Havana isn't just gold or silver; it's the flavor of life! Just look at those fruits—some of the best in the Caribbean."

After leaving the market, they strolled towards La Catedral de la Habana. "This cathedral," Victor began, "is not just a place of worship. It's a symbol of resilience, built amidst the challenges of our colonial past. It stands tall, reminding us that faith can weather any storm."

As they admired the intricate Baroque architecture, Elias marveled, "It truly is magnificent."

"Indeed! And speaking of storms, let me tell you about our military presence," Victor continued, leading Elias towards the barracks. "Havana has been a military stronghold, defending against not just pirates but rival colonial powers. They've had their share of drama, let me tell you!"

As the sun began to dip toward the horizon, casting a golden hue over the city, Elias felt a bittersweet twinge in his heart. The vibrant spirit of Havana, with its rich history and lively culture, was captivating, yet he knew his time in the New World was coming to an end. Soon, he would be leaving this place for good, setting sail for home in Baghdad.

"Victor," he said, "the Governor General urged me to return to Spain with him. So I'm cutting my stay in the Americas short."

"Really?" said Victor. "But I hear you have a promising chance to make a fortune in silver here."

"It's more important to accompany the Governor General," said Elias. "He has to return under difficult circumstances, and I want to help, if I can, to advocate for him."

"You are a loyal man."

Elias, turning to his guide with gratitude in his eyes, said, "thank you for the incredible journey through different parts of the New World. Your insights have opened my eyes to so much more than I could have imagined."

Victor smiled, his expression genuine. "It was my pleasure, Elias. The stories of this land are best shared with those eager to listen. I wish you safe travels back to Baghdad."

Elias nodded, feeling a sense of camaraderie. "And I wish you all the best in your future adventures here."

With that, they clasped hands, a gesture of goodwill and mutual respect. As Elias walked away, the weight of his departure settled in, but he carried with him the memories of a vibrant city and the friendships forged along the way. He took one last look at the bustling streets, the colorful buildings, and the shimmering bay, knowing he would forever cherish this chapter of his life.

Chapter 31

Elias' Final Destination

When Elias was ready to depart for Spain, he received nine cases of sugar and jars of jam in exchange for his gifts. He booked passage on a ship from Caracas for 350 piasters and set sail once more. Elias and his fellow travelers reached the island of Lucaya [Bahamas] and encountered severe sea turbulence generated by heavy winds, which lasted for eleven days. The heavy winds scattered the ships across the surface of the sea. Elias and the others felt overwhelmed with distress and grief. After eleven days, the sea calmed down with God's intervention, and all the scattered ships assembled once again. At night, they lit lanterns to avoid straying and getting lost, as well as to prevent collisions with one another. Finally, a favorable wind arose, and Elias and his companions resumed their course towards Cádiz. Twelve days later, they sighted land at dawn, and the wind remained helpful until midday.

Elias and his fellow travelers entered the harbor of Cádiz safely. The warships of the king of France were anchored outside the harbor, with warships of the king of Spain opposite them. As Elias' ship sailed between these two rows of warships, they saluted them with cannon fire, and both the French and Spanish warships returned the salute. This was followed by the two sides bombarding each other, with smoke accumulating like clouds. Elias and his companions then entered the harbor and dropped anchor.

The next day, friends from the town came out in rowboats and took them to land. The president's orders prompted Elias, the council head, and others to transport their unopened luggage to shore, bypassing the customary inspection process.

Ten days later, Elias went to Seville to recover two thousand piasters he had loaned the captain of the ship so he could buy what his ship needed. However, when the captain arrived in Cádiz, his ship was seized because he owed thirty thousand piasters to the church of Seville. Elias went there to lodge a complaint. The president decided in his favor, stating that they should pay the two thousand owed to Elias since the ship wouldn't have made it back without that loan. They paid Elias the money, and he then went to Cádiz and booked passage on a Dutch ship to travel to Rome. In his company were two Armenian servants.

Elias had brought with him from the West Indies four parrots that could talk like human beings. He also brought a silver candelabrum of rare workmanship, worth 1,450 piasters. Elias offered this candelabrum to the pope and the church of the Propaganda Fide. When the cardinals beheld it, they were greatly pleased with the delicateness of its craftsmanship. At that moment, Pope Innocent XI, a man of righteous deeds, granted Elias appointments that he felt unworthy of.

Although Elias wanted to return to his native land, upon arriving in Rome, he informed the Propaganda Fide that he would be killed if he returned home. Instead, he offered his talents to the Vatican. In March 1688, he represented Spanish Bishop Antonio de León, who was unable to undertake the required visita ad limina. By October 1691, Elias was still in Rome, requesting an audience with Pope Innocent XII, possibly to remain relevant to the Propaganda Fide's efforts to engage with the Church of the East. Around this time, he also contributed to the publication of an Arabic prayer book for the Propaganda Fide, with assistance from Andrawus ibn Abdallah. The last mention of Elias in the Propaganda Fide archives is from 1694, indicating he was then living in Spain. It's uncertain whether or not he ever returned to Mesopotamia.

The End

www.ingramcontent.com/pod-product-compliance
Lightning Source LLC
Chambersburg PA
CBHW020936090426
42736CB00010B/1158